CREATING LIFE

THE ART OF
WORLD BUILDING

VOLUME I

RANDY ELLEFSON

ISBN: 978-1-946995-01-8 (CreateSpace paperback)
ISBN: 978-1-946995-08-7 (IngramSpark paperback)
ISBN: 978-1-946995-06-3 (IngramSpark hardcover)

DISCLAIMER

This book includes fictional passages. All names, characters, locations, and incidents are products of the author's imagination, or have been used fictitiously. Any semblance to actual persons living or dead, locales, or events is coincidental and not intended by the author.

CONTENTS

ACKNOWLEDGMENTS

Special thanks to Raoul Miller, Laura Scroggins,
and Anne Heiser for their input.

Edited by JJ Henke

Cover design by Deranged Doctor Designs

INTRODUCTION

Series like *Harry Potter, Star Trek, The Lord of the Rings*, and *Star Wars* are beloved for their intricate and detailed worlds. Each has made their creators famous, respected, and fabulously wealthy. They've generated billions in revenue across multiple industries, including books, movies, games, and endless merchandising. They're part of popular culture. How can you emulate such skill? This book series, *The Art of World Building*, will teach you how to create believable, imaginative, and hopefully lucrative worlds to improve your fantasy or science fiction career.

My first goal with this series is to provide you with tools to speed you along in what is often time-consuming work. My second aims to help you realize your dreams and make great choices. Whether you've built many worlds before, are in the middle of your first one now, or have never started, this series can help you achieve your objectives by providing:

- An examination of your goals, options, and how much of your attention each subject needs

- Detailed advice on the pros and cons of every approach and how to balance them
- Extensive research on real-world elements you should understand and utilize
- How and when to use analogues
- Thought-provoking questions to help you make informed decisions and stimulate imagination
- Classification of world building elements into related areas for clarity
- Practical examples illustrating potential results
- Ideas on organizing world building files for quick access and minimized redundancy
- Reusable templates to ensure consistency and thoroughness

The examples included in the text were created specifically for this guide and are not drawn from any setting I've created, except in rare instances. Where possible, well-known books, films, and TV shows have been cited as good examples that illustrate a point. With examples of what to avoid, I've usually avoided naming the work. Many of the examples and discussions herein can trigger ideas.

The book has a website where you can find additional resources and information on other volumes in this series. Visit http://www.artofworldbuilding.com.

WHERE TO START

The series, and chapters within each volume, can be read in any order but are arranged according to what might come first in a world's timeline. Gods, if real, precede humanoids, which precede undead humanoids, et al. But our creations can be invented in any order. In fact, crisscrossing back and forth between different subjects is part of the work. We might start with inventing gods before working on species, then update our gods based on what we've done with species. It's unusual, even unlikely, to invent something and then never revisit it.

Only you can decide where to begin, but it's recommended to take any idea and run with it, writing down whatever occurs to you. If there are problems with it, they can be fixed later as you update and improve upon it. If you haven't read a chapter in this book and have an idea for something that's covered here, go ahead and write down everything you're thinking. Stopping to read this might make the idea vanish. We can also get it into our heads that we must do something "right." This is a dangerous thought because it inhibits creativity, which is the lifeblood of all art, including world building. It's better to jot down a poor idea and fix it later than to stall, research how it could be done, get overwhelmed, and then forget it or lose interest.

Doing it "right" is itself "wrong" much of the time, as there are seldom rules that cannot be bent and even broken. All advice, whether found in this series or another, is best stated in an open-ended manner and taken as food for thought rather than as a gospel that must be followed. If you disagree with anything written here or elsewhere, good for you. Deciding not to do something, or going about it a different way, still adds clarity to our process and results.

So where do you start? Where your heart lies.

ABOUT ME

By profession I'm a software developer, but I've been writing fantasy fiction since 1988 and building worlds just as long, mostly one planet called Llurien. Yes, I am crazy. But I love what I do. I didn't intend to work on it for so long, but when life has prevented me from writing, I've worked on Llurien. I've done everything in these chapters and authored two hundred thousand words of world building in my files. Llurien even has its own website now at http://www.llurien.com. I've written six novels and over a dozen short stories over the years, and have just begun my publishing career with a novella that you can read for free (see below).

I'm also a musician with a degree in classical guitar; I've released three albums of instrumental rock, one classical guitar CD, and a disc of acoustic guitar instrumentals. You can learn more, hear songs, and see videos at my main website, http://www.randyellefson.com.

FREE BOOK

If you'd like to see a free sample of my own world building efforts in action, anyone who joins my fiction newsletter mailing list receives a free eBook of *The Ever Fiend (Talon Stormbringer)*. Please note there's also a separate newsletter for *The Art of World Building*, though both can be joined on the same signup form. Just check the box for each at http://www.randyellefson.com/newsletter.

DISCLAIMERS

World building is defined as the act of creating an imaginary world. While that suggests an entire planet, the result is often one continent or less. By world building, I don't mean using pre-existing ideas and putting your own spin on them, such as reimagining Greek gods in modern or ancient times, or writing an alternate reality of Earth. While such approaches are fine, that's not what this series is about, though such creators may still find the series useful.

I've omitted the science behind any real or imagined technology (like the warp drive from *Star Trek*) because other books on these subjects exist. While I've included some details to help you create life forms with appropriate features, the information is tailored to world building uses. The guide focuses on being realistic about imagining new worlds while not being overly technical. Something like plate tectonics is discussed in volume two because it impacts the formation of mountains, but the details of subduction zones are seldom relevant for us when drawing mountain ranges, for example.

While some authors prefer the term "races" to "species," I've used the latter term throughout most of the series except for the section in this volume discussing the merits of both terms. This book uses "SF" to abbreviate science fiction. SF is broadly defined herein as a setting with technology far in excess of current capabilities. Fantasy is loosely defined in this series as a setting using magic, knights, and lacking modern technology. As a stylistic point, to avoid writing "he/she," I've also opted for "he" when discussing someone who could be either gender.

Since I am an author, and primarily write fantasy, the series is admittedly weighted in this direction, but whether you're in the gaming industry, a screenwriter, a hobbyist, or write science fiction, much of the three volumes can help you anyway. I just don't claim to have covered every last element despite my attempts to be reasonably comprehensive. If you have suggested topics you feel should be covered, feel free to contact me at mail@randyellefson.com about updates for later editions.

THE CHAPTERS

What follows is a brief summary of what's included in each chapter in volume one, *Creating Life*.

CHAPTER 1—WHY BUILD A WORLD?

While world building is expected in many genres of fantasy and SF, we must decide how many worlds to build. This will depend on our career plans and goals. Learn the advantages and disadvantages of building one world per story vs. one world for many stories, and when to take each approach. Sometimes doing both is best, allowing for greater depth in one world but the option to step away to keep things fresh. Using analogues can help us create believable societies quickly but has pitfalls that can be avoided. Do you have the ability to create many interesting worlds, and will they have enough depth to make the effort worth it?

CHAPTER 2—CREATING GODS

Our species will invent gods to believe in even if we don't invent them, so we may need some deities for people to reference in dialogue, whether praying or swearing. In SF, belief in gods may still exist despite, or even because of, advances in science. In fantasy, priests often call on a god to heal someone, and this requires having invented the gods. Pantheons offer advantages over a lone god, including dynamic relationships between them and the species. Half gods and demigods are other options that help us create myths and legends to enrich our world, especially if gods can be born, die, or be visited in their realm.

Myths about how the gods or species came to exist help people understand the purpose of their lives and what awaits them in death. Symbols, appearance, patronage, and willingness to impact the lives of their species all color a pantheon and world. Gods also create places people can visit or items that can fall into the wrong hands, offering possibilities for stories.

CHAPTER 3—CREATING A SPECIES

Audiences are familiar with using "race" to distinguish between humanoids, especially in fantasy, but "species" may be a more appropriate term. This chapter explores the meaning and implications of both words, with some examples of which one to use, when, and why.

Creating a species is challenging and time consuming, but the risks and rewards can be navigated and achieved, respectively. This chapter helps us decide on our goals and if the effort is worth it. SF writers might have little choice but to create species because there are no public domain species available like the elves, dwarves, and dragons of fantasy. The benefits of creating something different can outweigh the investment and help our work stand out.

An invented species must compete with legendary ones like elves, dwarves, and dragons; this chapter helps us achieve this. Starting with habitat helps us decide on physical adaptations that affect their minds, outlook, and society, and what a typical settlement might be like and even whether or not they live in jointly formed settlements. Their disposition affects their relationships with other species but can also limit their usefulness to us unless steps are taken to avoid this. Characteristics like intelligence, wisdom, and dexterity all play a role in how they can be used in our work, as does their society and world view, both affected by a history we can invent to integrate them with our world. Their familiarity with the supernatural and technology influences their prominence and how they compare to other life.

CHAPTER 4—CREATING WORLD FIGURES

Villains, heroes, and more give our characters admired or despised individuals who've shaped the world and inspired them. Using Earth analogues can speed the invention of such world figures, though it's best to change some details to obfuscate the similarities. Living figures can provide ongoing usefulness but the deceased can cast a long shadow, too. Their possessions can be just as famous and offer opportunities for our characters to find something helpful or dangerous. Family, friends, and enemies also provide ongoing possibilities for their life to impact our current characters.

CHAPTER 5—CREATING MONSTERS

The difference between monsters, species, and animals is largely sophistication and numbers. Many monsters are created by accidents that turn an existing species or animal into something else, but sometimes monsters are created on purpose. In the latter case it's especially important to decide who caused this. A monster's habitat has an impact on its usefulness and sets the stage for creating atmosphere and characterization that will largely define our audience's experience with it. Its motivation in life, or in our work, also determines what it does and the sort of trouble it's causing for our species.

CHAPTER 6—CREATING PLANTS AND ANIMALS

In fantasy, creating plants and animals is optional due to expectations that the world is very Earth-like, but in SF that takes place away from Earth, audiences are more likely to expect new ones. It takes less time to create these than other life in this book, but we'll want to consider our time investment, how often our setting will be used, whether our creations impact our work and the impression it creates, and whether the desire to do something unique and new is worthwhile for both us and our audience.

Plants and animals are classified into categories, such as cycads, conifers, and flowering plants, and amphibians, birds, fish, mammals, and reptiles. The lifecycle of the former and the behavior of the latter help distinguish them and can be used to propel or inhibit stories involving them. While we may have purposes for them as an author, our world's inhabitants have them, too, such as decoration and medicinal uses for plants, and domestication, sports, guards, pets and transportation for animals. Both can be used for food and materials to enrich life and our world.

CHAPTER 7—CREATING UNDEAD

Many types of undead already exist and are public domain, and it's challenging to invent something new. Undead are often classified by appearance and behavior, but it is also their origins and how they can be destroyed that will help distinguish our undead from pre-existing types. The two basic ones are those with a body, like zombies, and those without, like ghosts. Those with a body might have a soul or not. We can decide on the mental faculties of our undead by deciding if the mind goes with the soul, but there are other factors that can impair the minds and even emotional states of undead. All of these affect behavior, as do their origins, goals, and what they're capable of.

TEMPLATES AND NEWSLETTER

Effective world building requires having written down details about the created world. To help you organize and jumpstart your efforts, each volume in this series includes templates in the appendices. This volume includes seven: gods, species, monsters, world figures (heroes, villains, and more), plants, animals, and undead.

Rather than typing these up yourself, you can download these templates for free by joining the newsletter for *The Art of World Building*. As each volume is published, whether you've bought the book or not, subscribers will automatically receive an email with links to download the templates as Microsoft Word files, which you can repeatedly use.

Visit http://www.artofworldbuilding.com/newsletter/

THE PODCAST

The Art of World Building podcast expands on the material within the series. The additional examples offer world builders more insight into ramifications of decisions. You can hear the podcast, read transcripts, and learn more about the episodes.

Visit http://www.artofworldbuilding.com/podcasts.

CREATING PLACES
(VOLUME 2)

The life we create needs to originate from somewhere on a planet: an ocean, a continent, in a land feature (like a forest or mountain range), in a kingdom, or in a settlement. *Creating Places (The Art of World Building, #2)* goes into detail about inventing such locations and figuring out how long it takes to travel between them by various forms of locomotion: foot, horse, wagon, dragon, wooden ship, spaceship, and more. The overall rules of our world are also considered, along with inventing time, history, various places of interest, and how to draw maps. We can start our work with any one of those subjects and crisscross between places and life, for one often impacts the other.

CULTURES AND BEYOND
(VOLUME 3)

Everything not covered in the first two volumes lies within the finale, *Cultures and Beyond (The Art of World Building, #3)*. This includes creating culture, language, religions, military groups, the supernatural, technology, magic items, names, and even mundane items like a monetary system. Much of this work ties together our life forms and places. These are the things we comment on most during a story and which our characters consider. Without them, no world building project is complete.

1

———•••———

WHY BUILD A WORLD?

Some people do it for fun, some do it for their stories, and some might do it from a sense of obligation (it's expected in their genre), but world building is always voluntary. We can easily craft a story using standard staples like elves and dragons, castles and wizards, or anything else we've all seen before. But if you wanted to repeat what everyone else has done, this book wouldn't have attracted your attention. We can be creative in more than just storytelling. We can do more than slap together a new species after only a little development time because we aren't going to use it much or dive into details about it.

We've all seen something new that made us wish we'd thought of it. We've all wanted our work to stand out. And who hasn't gotten a little bored with those available, public domain ideas? They're overused because everyone can use them. Why not create something unique, something that makes our world shine brightly?

The answer is that it's not easy. It can be time consuming. They are so many things to consider. And if no one likes what we've built after countless hours of blood, sweat, and tears, we've wasted all of that time and effort. Failure costs us respect. People stop enjoying our work. Maybe they write a snarky review online. The more risk we take, the greater our odds of failure.

And the better our odds of being brilliant.

The Art of World Building series ensures you do the latter. It's designed to help you avoid pitfalls and improve the quality of your ideas so you can create a memorable world that's respected, fascinating, and a huge asset to your works. If you're one of the lucky few, there might even be extensive merchandising opportunities if people are captivated with your world. But let's not get ahead of ourselves or leave all of this to chance.

USING ANALOGUES

Do we really need to build a world? Only if our story takes place somewhere other than Earth. But that world can be so Earth-like that it's essentially Earth with another name. This is the easiest approach with the lowest amount of risk. Unfortunately, it's also the least interesting. This is what's referred to as an analogue: something that has a corresponding version on Earth.

For example, maybe we invent a small island country called Xenoi where ritual suicide is accepted, honor is cherished over life, expert swordsman use special swords, women are subservient, everyone has black hair, fish and rice are diet staples, and there's an emperor. How far did you get through that before you realized Xenoi is Japan? Which elements would you remove so that it's not so obvious?

We should make changes to our analogues so they aren't easily recognized.

The Rule of Three

When using an analogue, strive to change the source in at least three significant ways. Focus on the most prominent aspects and alter some, or make a longer list and decide what matters to keep and what doesn't. If you have no specific use for a trait that really identifies the analogue, remove it.

For example, an elf lives in the forest, has pointed ears, and disrespects humans. Do we need the pointed ears? Are they serving a purpose we can't live without? Why not ditch the negative attitude? Leaving them in forests might be good, but maybe they should be more wide ranging. This exercise can be done to everything else in this book series. Follow the rule of three and fewer people will recognize your analogues.

What's In a Name?

More than you think.

Let's say I invent a world that features a horse with an extra pair of legs. Next I incorporate a poisonous yellow tomato as well as a lion of superior intelligence. Then I call these objects horse, tomato, and lion. Would you remember the differences or picture the traditional versions?

There's a kind of mental inertia to a known term; it suggests familiarity, which in turn overwrites our memory of a different detail in the book we're reading. For example, if a horse is described as having six legs the first time it's mentioned, but that detail never arises over the next hundred times the creature appears, readers completely forget it has two more legs.

This issue is less true in a visual medium—we're reminded of the difference every time the creature appears—but in books, we'll have to keep reminding people, which feels like unnecessary exposition and housekeeping (for us and the audience). If we have to keep calling it a "six-legged horse," that encumbrance isn't much better. If we don't call it a horse, but describe it in such a way that people think, "Oh, it's just a horse with two more legs," is that an improvement? More importantly, unless the alteration matters in some way, why do it at all? It does make the world more alien, which is a fine goal.

Another issue we can face is inappropriately using a known term. There are expectations about what a word means, and while we have some creative license to make things our own and put a new spin on something, there's a limit to how much liberty we can take before we cause a negative reaction. An obvious example would be calling a seven-foot-tall humanoid a dwarf (unless all other humanoids are considerably taller than that). In a visual medium, we must be especially careful not to be too obvious with an analogue. I recently saw a movie where characters spoke of goblins. I formed an expectation of what I'd see. Imagine my surprise when the goblin turned out to look like a gorilla with horns and a love of gold. It even moved and behaved like a gorilla. My expectations were defied in a way that jarred me right out of the story.

These factors should be considered when deciding if we should use another name. A new word also carries some risk. Authors may need to present a longer description to an audience. What we're describing needs to be firmly imprinted on the reader's mind so that little more than the term is needed later. We might use the occasional mention of a characteristic, preferably during action involving that feature so it doesn't seem like a reminder.

World builders can decide based on how many changes we've made to the analogue. The more changes we've made, the more our creation warrants a new name. How to create names is covered in *Cultures and Beyond*.

HOW MANY WORLDS?

ONE VS. MANY

Since world building takes time, we should consider how many worlds we might build over the course of our career and whether it makes sense to build a world per story (twenty worlds for twenty stories), just one world for all [twenty] stories, or a mixture of both. Or neither. Let's look at the pros and cons of each approach.

ONE WORLD FOR ONE STORY

Creating a world for each story has some advantages. We build only what we need for that tale, so it takes less time. We don't have to think through so many items. We're not tied to that world indefinitely; if our audience doesn't like it, or we grow tired of it, or something just doesn't seem to be working, we were done with it anyway. Those creators who aren't sure how much writing they'll do can test the world building waters and learn if it's something they enjoy. If we're a novice at world building and it shows in early work, we can learn and move on rather than having to fix those mistakes. If we have a more experimental concept that takes greater risks with an audience supporting it, we've risked less.

This approach has disadvantages as well. Skimping on world building could cause an under-developed or less interesting world. It can be less unique, too, if we use staples like elves, dwarves, and dragons. It takes considerable work to invent species that favorably compare to those. If we do a lot of work but only use it once, is it worth it? We'll have to repeat much of that work every time we invent another world. This could cause world building fatigue when we're on our twentieth world. The risk of repeating ourselves also rises. If a story becomes very popular and our audience demands more, we might find that our less developed concepts have caused problems we struggle to resolve in later works.

ONE WORLD FOR MANY STORIES

The alternative is to build one world for use on those twenty books. Just doing it once means not repeating ourselves. Greater depth and realism can be created by inventing more detail, which is needed to make new concepts, like species, more believable. This approach becomes worthwhile if we'll use the setting for years. If we invent new life and use only those, we're no longer bound by the expectations that familiar species cause. We have freedom to follow our own rules. Our books will stand out, and if the setting is popular, this alone can draw fans back with each new product released. We might even be able to license the world for product development, from action figures to role-playing spin-offs.

This much attention to detail is a considerable time investment, which *The Art of World Building* will reduce. We need a diverse world to avoid audience boredom over so many tales, and this requires months, even years of development. During that time, we'll benefit from friends who are willing to provide feedback on the world we've created, but this is hard to get. People want to comment on a story, not on our world building. If we know other world building authors, they might help and are our best resource. If we never get published, we never reach an audience and have arguably wasted time, but having multiple stories to set in that world mitigates this, as does the ability to self-publish. Time spent on this is also time not spent on our writing craft. World building fatigue can creep in from inventing so many things, but everything is optional and some elements have higher priorities than others.

On the surface, creating one setting per book may involve less effort at the time, but if we have to create a dozen worlds over the years, is that more or less work than one more detailed, reusable setting?

THE HYBRID

We can split the difference—create one planet that's intended for many stories while also creating less developed ones for single stories. This hybrid approach is the best of both worlds. We might need a break from our "main" world (for lack of a better term) or just want to do something different or new once again. We can utilize a single-use world for more extreme risks, keeping our main world more accessible.

If we create a main world to use many times, a mixed approach will ease the upfront time investment. This is discussed in more detail in volume three, *Cultures and Beyond*, "Getting Started" chapter. What we can do is create our continents in rough form, then the gods of that whole world, and any species, animals, and plants that are found mostly everywhere. Then focus on a continent and some nations on the large scale and some basic history, including wars and animosities. We'll also need a major city or two in every kingdom. At that point, we've created a basic framework for the rest. As needed when writing a story, we can flesh out details of any given city.

At later times, we can develop other continents, cities, and add more monsters and other creatures as we go along. If we have a new book series, we can set it on the world we've created but in another kingdom or continent we haven't used much, or even in another time period. And yet we still have our species, our gods, or a system of magic. We can reuse much of what we've already done.

HOW TO DECIDE

Consider how passionate you are about world building. If you're an author, your primary goal is telling stories. Will you be satisfied with showing your originality in the story more than the setting? Is there a risk you'll get so involved in world building that you'll seldom get around to telling those stories? Authors are well known for finding excuses not to write despite wanting to write. Will this become one? Every minute on this is a minute you could've spent on your writing craft or building an audience. Where does your heart lie?

It's also important to consider how long you intend your career to be. If you're a "lifer" and will write for decades in a genre requiring world building, then expending a lot of effort makes more sense than for someone who wants to give writing a shot and will bow out after failure, or even modest success. If you know that's you, why invest tons of time, even if you love it? Fiction is a speculative field, but writing a book at least produces a product to be sold; building a world seldom does.

Life intrudes on our time to write. This is truer for longer works like a novel. If we don't have time to write a novel this year, because we're in college, or just became a parent, or something else, we can spend time inventing a setting instead. A novel takes months of continuous work to stay involved, but world building can be done in a few minutes here and there. In my case, I spent most of a decade unable to write due to first college and then an injury that made writing difficult; in the meantime, I built an enormous amount for my main world. The younger me gave the older me a great gift.

HOW MANY WORLDS ARE IN YOU?

Do world builders have the ability to create more than one great world? Theoretically, yes. Do you? Creative people try to avoid repeating themselves. The more specific an idea, the more sense it makes to exclude it from a second world. Having dragons on both worlds is okay, but if the first world is dominated by dragons who only breathe fire, cast no magic, and won't let anyone ride them, then repeating that in another world makes us look like we have no imagination; the dreaded "formula" accusation will get hurled at us. With each world created, we further restrict ourselves. Soon we're out of ideas. We could solve that by being generic all the time, but then what's the point of world building?

A CAVEAT

If the first story we publish in a world begins a series, audiences may/will expect any subsequent stories set on that planet to have some connection to that initial one. This likely originates from this being what authors frequently do. If we defy this expectation, there may be some backlash. We can avoid this expectation by publishing unrelated stories on that world *before* a series there. One problem with that solution is that if we're self-publishing, it's widely believed that our careers will do best if we publish a series because readers gobble up subsequent books, so perhaps self-publishing a few unrelated short stories or a novella gets us past all of this. Or we can just ignore the issue.

A QUESTION OF DEPTH

A single, detailed world provides a richer, more diverse, immersive experience for an audience, but we must remember that they want a story, even in gaming. World building is always subservient to this, and yet when we spend many hours doing it, we're tempted to include more of what we've created than is required for our story. We're too close to our work. It can be prudent to take breaks from world building and remember that it isn't the ultimate goal.

Audiences don't want stories about our world building. They want stories about people and conflicts. These should be layered within our setting, not used as an excuse to show off what we've invented. There are ways to achieve this.

For example, when I created the Coiryn Riders, a group of military horsemen distinct from knights, I went overboard. I ended up with a fifteen-thousand-word file of details on their ranks, advancement, training, usages, equipment, and more. I could never get all this across in an average novel even if I wanted to (and I don't). But there are many ways I can use them.

I could have a lead character become a Coiryn Rider and show his rise through the ranks over the course of a novel series, revealing many details about the horsemen and what it's like to be one. As minor characters, they also serve as heralds, so one might be tasked with traveling alone through hostile lands. They are supposed to be given safe passage, which provides an opportunity for a King's Herald to be killed by an enemy power, inciting war. One might use his military skills as part of an adventuring group I'm featuring. I can have my main characters encounter a group of Coiryn Riders on nearing a city, revealing that the riders routinely patrol perimeters, or in their role as heralds, deliver warnings of nearby threats. They are also cavalry in army war scenes.

That's several possible uses. I wouldn't want to try jamming all of this into one story. Instead, I can spread it out across many tales over the course of my career. By having worked out so many details in advance, I run little risk of contradicting myself with later works set on Llurien, a problem that inventing/publishing piece by piece exposes us to.

The Coiryn Riders were not invented for a specific tale. They were invented for their own sake as something that exists on Llurien, filling a role or need. When I'm assembling a cast or story idea, I include them if they can help me achieve my story goals. And when there's no use for them, they don't get a mention. I'm not tempted to include extraneous world building. I know I'm going to write many stories in my career and sooner or later I'll show many facets of these horsemen, collectively painting both a broad and a detailed picture. Doing so arguably creates the greatest depth of all. And it prevents me from walloping my audience with a ton of unnecessary info at any given time.

When we create a world to tell a single story, we don't have that option. We might be more tempted to ramble on about our world building. Or we don't invent those things at all because we won't be using them, which predisposes our world to lack depth. But we need to have a well-realized world (just not go too far), for the same reason we invent character backstory—it helps flesh out our depiction of the world, and helps our readers to understand it.

THE PROBLEM OF EXPOSITION

The objection to exposition is that authors cause a loss of momentum when they stop the story to explain a setting or even a character, then resume on the other side. Authors of older books sometimes wrote pages upon pages of exposition; I usually skip over this. Modern audiences expect a story to keep moving. I've had beta-readers give me grief about exposition as short as a four-sentence paragraph. This seems a little harsh to me, and you'll have to use your own judgment. Whether or not an explanation is too much is a personal choice. Keep in mind when inventing something that requires explanation that many readers will skip these passages, or an editor might strike them entirely.

How is an author to get across needed information? That's a writing question more than a world building one, but an old standby is the ignorant character who keeps asking what something means only to have another character explain it to them. Overusing this is a poor style choice. The technique is especially prominent in films without a narrator, though some shows use heavy voiceovers to explain things.

Like it or not, some exposition will always be needed. We just don't want a death certificate for our stories to have "Death by Exposition" on the cause of death line.

SHOW VS. TELL

One way around exposition is to reveal world building details as an integral part of a story. For example, my story "The Garden of Taria" exists so I can reveal an aspect of a humanoid species (querra). However, that's my goal as an author. It's not a reader-centric goal of a story about characters, which is what we want.

So I created a character, Taria, who seeks refuge from a chaotic world in the ordered sanctuary of her home. The querra keeps invading her house whilst helping himself to her possessions and food. He makes a mess everywhere and doesn't respect property. All of this is what I wanted to show. Their arguments reveal querran outlook as I'd desired, but this doesn't come as exposition. It's dialogue and behavior. Their conflict causes both characters, and maybe the reader, to question human ideas on property, possession, capitalism, and wealth. In other words, I'm showing this world building element, not telling it. The story is about characters and issues, achieved with world building.

And *that's* what we want.

OTHER METHODS

We can also include more details in a glossary with each published work. Since perusing it is optional, readers with greater curiosity will do so while those who don't care are freed from exposition overkill. Tolkien did something similar with *The Lord of the Rings*, which includes multiple appendices.

A related solution is to create a website all about our world, linking to it from our glossary or even the text of our stories. Each time a new item is mentioned in a tale, the word is a hyperlink to the corresponding page on the website. This is also optional for our readers, who may love being able to do this; they might also be annoyed/distracted by the sight of a hyperlink in a novel unless this sort of thing becomes common.

A website might be overkill unless we're a successful writer, but it can help invest readers in our world and possibly draw in new ones. The size of the website is up to us. It can just be a few pages or a longer glossary associated with our book's page. For me, the online version is the master glossary, the one in a book being far shorter and tailored to that story. For examples, you can see mine at Llurien.com.

THE VALUE OF INFLUENCES

During world building, we can become so focused on inventing something new that we try not to be influenced by anything we've seen before. While this is admirable, we can inadvertently deny ourselves something precisely because someone has done it, which means we're still being influenced. True freedom to invent means not worrying about similarities at all and using every possible good idea, with the caveat that we must avoid copyright infringement.

For example, I avoided inventing an underground species because I figured they'd just be dwarves by another name, because they'd be short. They have to dig most passages and homes, and this will inhibit their vertical growth, or they'll all have stooped backs. I let myself be influenced in the negative, avoiding something useful until I realized that a dwarf is far more than just height and habitat.

Aspire to create a species that looks and lives however you want them to. If a physical adaptation is based on habitat, this is good. If it makes sense for our forest-dwelling species to have pointed ears and slanted eyes, then so be it, even though elves are like that. Incidentally, pointed ears don't have a biological basis and don't improve hearing; such criteria can help us eliminate or add features. When you notice that you want to do something that reminds you of someone else's creation, question why theirs is like that. If the feature doesn't make sense, ditch it. The most powerful influences are the ones we don't even realize we have.

Question everything.

2

CREATING GODS

Whether we write fantasy or science fiction, chances are sooner or later we'll need a god or gods. At the least, our characters might want to pray, swear, threaten damnation, or utter thanks. And when someone is born, dies, or reaches a milestone, gods are often praised.

Gods are typically credited with the reason for everything existing, but starting our world building with them is optional. Our gods can be real or wishful thinking, but in fantasy and SF, they are typically portrayed as real and taking an active role in the lives of the world's residents. Different religions spring up from different beliefs about even a single shared god, so before we can create religions, decide on deities.

Did the gods create our world on purpose or was it a byproduct of a "big bang" origin, and they stumbled upon it? Did they shape the land or just let it do its thing over millennia? Are they active, causing seasons, night/day, and winds, or do they just manipulate these forces?

Appendix 1 is a template for creating a god. It includes

more comments and advice, and an file can be down-loaded for free by signing up for the newsletter at http://www.artofworldbuilding.com/newsletter/.

IN SCIENCE FICTION

In SF, characters may travel between many worlds, each having a pantheon, which is not to say that we need an extensively developed pantheon for each world. Rather, a general feel for the presence of religion and actual gods appearing can be all that we need, plus a few names.

There's an idea that science kills religion, the premise being that the more scientific discoveries are made, the less need we have of religion to explain things. While there's some truth to this, religion shouldn't be ignored. People still often believe in deities. Some might say that less educated, more rural people fall into this category, but many of our greatest scientists believe in God. Writing SF on possibly highly-developed worlds doesn't absolve us from inventing religion, which will never really go away. Our characters can live/arrive on a world dominated by religion despite science.

One way to work religion into SF is to consider world view issues. Planet-hopping characters may believe that gods created the universe and therefore these deities will also rule other planets. Discovering on arrival that no one's heard of those gods will cause distress. They may try to claim the new planet's god X is really their home planet's god Y. Or they may be so incensed that they try to wipe out the inhabitants of this wayward planet. Or convert them. Christian missionaries tried to spread God's word around Earth, so why not do the same on a planetary level?

Whether the gods are real or not is another matter to consider. If real, are they happy with a species gaining so much power that they can leave the world the gods created for them? If they created the universe, maybe they're okay with it because those gods rule the other planets as well. If the gods didn't create the universe and only rule their area of it, maybe they encourage our characters to colonize other worlds and galaxies, or the peaceful lives they live are shattered by alien invaders coming to convert them. Is there a proxy war going on between these gods and those of other worlds? Our gods could provide the technologies being used to travel.

In SF, sometimes the gods are actually advanced aliens masquerading as gods, as in *Stargate SG-1*. This can be useful for having "gods" that can be killed, perhaps to the surprise of the mortals they rule. The discovery of the truth can be psychologically powerful. We'll need to figure out where the aliens came from and why they're doing this.

IN FANTASY

In fantasy, gods often put in appearances that leave little doubt that they exist. In antiquity, there are numerous myths of Norse and Greek gods being jealous of humans, tormenting, killing, and having children with us. The Christian god is the one who keeps quiet. We can choose either approach, but gods who affect events are more useful. Their followers can be the ones impacting life, whether these are your main characters or their enemies. A common use for gods is to have a priest lay hands on wounded people and ask their god to heal them. We need deities for this. A developed pantheon helps us flesh out the priest character's personality as we decide who they pray to.

If our world has multiple humanoid species, do we want each species to have their own gods or to share all of them? The latter reduces the numbers we must create, but the former allows for more variety. Each species can have their own creation and end-of-world myths, for example. We might invent gods that are tailored to a species, rather than all gods being universal and therefore less specific. To minimize the quantity invented, we can decide each species only has a few gods, not twenty each. We might also decide that some gods are universal while others are more tailored to a species. This works well if a subgroup of gods invented that species, their combined attributes influencing the result. That species can worship all the gods but have more allegiance for their creators.

PANTHEONS

A pantheon is a mythological collection of gods. They are often related by familial ties and recognized by the culture that invented them but not usually by others. While creating multiple gods is more work, dynamic relationships among deities is more entertaining and can drive plot. We can start with a list of traits, such as truth, courage, love, hate, patience, curiosity, peace, greed, fear, sloth, deceit, and wrath. We can use phenomena like gods of storms, war, and death. We don't have to choose one approach or the other, but mixing them could make our pantheon seem random and not well thought out. One solution is to decide that traits lead to phenomenon, or vice versa. For example, the god of wrath becomes the god of storms. This is expanded on further in the last section of this chapter.

A pantheon allows characters to show personality by the god(s) they pray to, especially for priests. As our characters investigate catacombs, ancient ruins, or a modern megalopolis, they will see symbols of the gods, encounter overzealous priests, or even visit a theocratic society. These elements can affect the decisions they make, such as not entering a given room due to the symbol of the god of torture on it. Even unrecognized symbols from an unknown pantheon can be useful for creating an unsettling feeling.

Our pantheon might have more than one afterlife (covered in *Cultures and Beyond, The Art of World Building, #3*), whether it's as simple as heaven and hell or more complicated, where different deities have conceived different rewards and punishment and oversee them personally. Deities can have a role in how people are judged, whether they can be redeemed, and if the living can visit the dead, or vice versa. When we assign gods different roles, we can create conflict in how (and if) they choose to do their jobs.

A pantheon is often not organized in any particular way, with the exception of familial relationships, should they exist, but if we assign certain traits to every god, we can group them that way. For example, maybe every god is associated with a season, element, or color. This causes multiple gods of spring, fire, or indigo. This may impact their ability to affect elements, their priests similarly affected. A god or priest of fire might suffer more from water-based attacks. Some people also organize their gods by good and evil.

POWER

Often, the gods of a pantheon are not equally powerful. If one or two are considered the parents of others, this can explain their greater strength. Or a few gods will be affiliated with more powerful subjects, like light and death. If the number of worshippers directly influences a god's power, this can also be used to determine their strength—and give a jealous god reason to kill off a rival's followers.

Some pantheons have gods, demigods, and half gods, the latter usually being human/god, though there's no reason you can't have a half elf/god instead. Or half ogre/god—such a person could wreak additional havoc or be more influential over peers, causing an uprising. Determine if these lesser beings exist, how they come about, and why. These are useful for lesser traits that we might still want a deity of.

CHILDREN

Parental relationships are sometimes cited as the reason for different power levels. This doesn't have to be. Human children, once grown, are no less powerful than their parents, so unless gods become increasingly powerful with time, like vampires supposedly do, there's little justification for this, unless…

Are children born at full power or did they need to grow into adulthood? The former offers opportunities to create stories of them learning to control their power. Children and adolescents make mistakes and test boundaries. Imagine what problems a budding god can cause. This is a good chance to create myths, attitudes, grudges, and infamous events or consequences for gods and species alike.

For example, perhaps a god inadvertently created a species that has something wrong with it. Maybe a deity cursed a group of one species, creating a new race. This could've been done to a species that another god admired, either to offend the god or retaliate for another offence.

Older gods may impose limits on younger ones just as parents do for teenagers, which can be a useful metaphor our characters refer to. How do these younger gods chafe at this? Is there an age at which the limits come off? Does something become possible at that age? Are these gods protected from something until then and then they're on their own to save themselves from some force known to harm deities? How long do the child gods take to reach adulthood?

DEMIGODS AND HALF GODS

Demigods can result from mating between gods or a god and a member of a mortal species, though some refer to the latter as half gods, which may live longer than the species but not be immortal. A demigod can be all god and immortal, perhaps just not as strong, but there really are no rules.

A demigod can result from a character who excelled at

something in life and became the demigod of that thing in death. A god of music might appoint a skilled singer the demigod/patron of singers after death. Demigods are often depicted as working for one or more gods, such as a messenger. Some might be neutral or they may take sides in godly and earthly disputes; if they did so in the past, maybe now the other side in that dispute doesn't trust them. Decide how much autonomy they enjoy. What happens if a demigod disobeys an order? Such thinking can lead to myths that enrich a pantheon.

RELATIONSHIPS

We can create relationships, familial or not, based on god traits. A god of love and a god of hate can be twins, as can the gods of life and death. The god of winter and demigod of snow can be parent and child. While these are a bit predictable, symmetry is appreciated and easier to remember. Gods can be friends and enemies, too. This often results from conflicts of character and desires, just like with people. If these boil over into arguments that become myths, this helps justify the intensity of bonding or resentment. Not every god in your pantheon needs details worked out, but a few will create the impression of depth we're after.

WHERE DO THEY LIVE?

Deciding where your gods live will have an impact on stories if your characters ever need to visit them. In theory, it shouldn't be easy to reach gods; otherwise, every guy with a cause will beg for help. A useful tradition to follow is that one must prove one's worthiness through an arduous trek to the god.

Do the gods live apart from each other or all together in a city? I recommend avoiding something as obvious as a mountain top because readers will be reminded of Mt.

Olympus. On the other hand, the god of the sea living underwater makes too much sense to ignore, but we can still have him do something less common, such as dwell on an island; after all, how is anyone supposed to visit him underwater, or is that what he's trying to avoid?

Are the gods in the mortal world, like your planet, or in a magical realm similar to an afterlife? What sort of guardians protect the path there? What price must someone pay, literally or figuratively, to get there and back? You can base your decisions on ideas from existing mythologies about travel to other dimensions, such as Charon, but a guy ferrying people across a dangerous river for a price is another idea that's too well-known to use without inducing eye rolling.

If the gods are believed to live in the sky, what happens in a world technologically advanced enough to explore the heavens and discover there are no gods up there? They would likely alter their beliefs to compensate for this. But it could be interesting if the gods are real and are indeed up there. Maybe this is the reason advanced technology was sought. There could be important questions the gods must be asked.

LIFESPAN

Where did your gods come from? "Nowhere" is a valid, if not entirely interesting, answer. On Earth, we don't talk much about where God came from so much as where *we* did. We can avoid this question altogether and few will question it. We don't actually need a reason, but something is usually better than nothing unless the idea doesn't hold up. We may never have a chance to mention it in stories anyway.

Our gods could've come from another world that they've abandoned or destroyed. Is your new planet their second or third chance to get it right? Maybe the gods are fleeing enemies, or they are the terror of the cosmos that other pantheons flee. Did they leave a planet full of life behind? That planet could be the one you're setting up now. If the gods abandoned a world, decide what's happening there now. Is that where Earth's God went? Is He too busy setting up other worlds to drop in?

Consider what the origins of your gods say or imply about them. In Greek mythology, the gods came from the giants before them, but if gods can be born, they can presumably be killed, too. If your gods can die, what happens when one does? Maybe the one who killed them can replace them. A magic or technological weapon might be needed to do it. Perhaps only other gods have the power to destroy one. Maybe they can only become injured. Or imprisoned—and what happens when this occurs? What kind of prison can hold a god? Decide where it is located, how is it guarded and by what. Does their influence over the world stop as long as they're locked up?

VULNERABILITY

There's an idea that stories about gods who can't be hurt or killed are not interesting because there's no risk to them. This has merit, but there are ways to injure someone other than physically. You can destroy their plans, offend their pride, and cause psychological trauma, all with consequences for the god and the offender. Don't be afraid to have gods with faults. The one God of Judaism, Islam, and Christianity is supposedly perfect—and therefore uninteresting?

We can make our gods vulnerable to magic items or various kinds of radiation, whether nature or technology causes it. A farmer with a spade shouldn't be able to kill a god unless that spade is magical. Decide what weapons can hurt deities and what the gods have done to find and destroy these, or if some gods are harboring them for eventual use on the others; they likely won't admit to this.

For a god to die of natural causes doesn't fit with our

concept of gods, so if you'd like some of them gone forever, you'll need a reason and event that your species are well aware of; a dead god is a powerful idea that might greatly disturb them. It suggests truly frightening foes are out there, unless the culprit was some sort of disease that only affects deities.

In some books, authors have a god sleeping or unconscious instead of dead, the eventual reawakening and possible consequences woven into a prophecy. How did this happen? Failed murder attempt? Poisoning? By who? What's gone wrong in the meantime? Is this god nefarious or benevolent? Do people long for the return or fear it? What is the god's religion doing to bring it about?

Can the gods hurt our species? Undoubtedly, unless we decide something's preventing them, such as a pact among them, a curse, or a powerful spell. Any of these would give some or all of them something to work against, giving them a story arc that might involve the species, some of whom might be helping or trying to hinder them. Is there an end-of-world doomsday that cannot take place as a result of what's happened? Maybe the species have found a way to thwart the end of all time, and the gods aren't amused.

MYTHOLOGY

A pantheon will have a mythology, whether it's featured heavily in stories or just mentioned by characters or in narration. To avoid exposition, incorporating the myths into a tale is the best way to mention them. This is one area we can stall on inventing, but creation myths and end-of-world myths are among the most important to work out; minor myths can be invented when needed. Even if our world doesn't have gods, these myths will exist, as our awareness of our own mortality has us contemplating the birth and death of everything, not just ourselves. Any story about incidents among the gods, or between gods and their species, can also become a myth people either believe or not.

CREATION MYTHS

Creation myths reveal a species' understanding of where they and the gods who created them originated. The question of "Why are we here?" is fundamental. If we've decided a subgroup of gods invented this species, why did they do this? What was the purpose? Were they unsatisfied with another species and created this one to solve a problem? Does that mean this new one has a task of wiping out the inferior predecessor? A superiority complex, racism (think white supremacy), and genocide are likely to result.

If the gods jointly created all species, especially at the same time, there may be a single creation myth instead of one per species. But there may be less purpose behind a wholesale invention of life other than to just do it. If there's no real reason, the species might invent stories to explain their existence, as we've done on Earth, where multiple myths exist across one species. We probably don't want multiple creation myths unless our story heavily features them; we can focus on just one universal myth.

The gods might have told everyone a story rather than let people invent one. But did the gods tell the truth or a modified version of it? There's more drama and conflict when people discover things are not quite what they believed; the more wrong we were, the more devastated we are. Our world could have a huge secret—the true origins of the gods and species. We can drop hints throughout a collection of stories and eventually have a powerful reveal in a longer work that re-imagines much of our previous work; this sort of thing must be planned to avoid contradicting ourselves.

There are justifications for lying gods. If they originated from the destruction of another being, maybe they don't want the species realizing the gods can be destroyed (under the right circumstances). If they are the ones who destroyed another being, maybe this wasn't as just or honorable as they'd like to believe. Any bad deed can suffice. If different worlds have different gods who war against each other, deity conflicts could result in attempts to protect their species, or themselves, through deceit or ignorance. The word "myth" implies falsehood, but if our gods are real, we can always opt for them to have told the truth. Some characters within a species will believe while others don't, the word myth still being applied.

Myths are imagined early in a civilization's development and have an oral tradition; even uneducated people know them. They often include supernatural beings, which means more than just our gods. The Greek gods had titans they fought with, for example. What beings might your gods have battled? Dragons? Any mythical creature from fantasy will do, if it is one of epic power.

The myth may include how the stars, moons, planets, and sun(s) came to be and which one is revolving around the others. Long ago, people thought the Earth was the center of the known universe, with the sun revolving around us. Is your species right about their place in the cosmos? They almost certainly are in SF but maybe not in fantasy. Some fantasy species may know the truth while the more ignorant ones may not.

Some people want to know that their lives are not a mistake, that there's a purpose to their existence and that of all mankind (or another species), and that their efforts to live well will be rewarded in life or death. And those who don't measure up will be punished. In this sense, a creation myth is often tied to an end-of-time myth. A species might be rationalizing their world view with a myth; we might need to invent some species first.

ANALOGUES

Earth provides many examples to leverage. Sometimes a god creates life in a dream or accidentally when something from their body falls to the earth and spawns life, whether this is tears, breast milk, another fluid, or their body somehow being dismembered or otherwise dying. A god can send an animal into a primordial ocean to dredge up enough earth to cause continents. Sometimes they just want to create order from chaos or nothingness. If there are two primeval gods (like earth and sky) who are separated, this sometimes causes life.

Life can be seen as emerging from a previous world, which can be literal or figurative; there's a metamorphosis occurring in which a higher state has been attained, and this current life will pass, too, as beings ascend again to another world in the next life. Sometimes the myth says that people have traveled here from afar, which can be a literal journey; this could be especially true in SF with planet-hopping characters, who might have also been driven from their original world, having an end of world myth to explain what happened.

END OF WORLD MYTHS

Our world also needs an end-of-time myth. This is often depicted as the culmination of many events that inevitably lead to the end of the world. This can be literal in the planet being destroyed, which fits with SF very well; maybe everyone is fleeing the planet on spaceships shortly before this foretold event. Or it happened long ago and a new reality is that this species (or many) is without a home; this has been done before but is still viable. In fantasy, tremendous magical power can render a world uninhabitable.

The end can be more figurative—life as people know it is over, but the world still physically exists. If the gods are destroyed but were responsible for granting magical or healing power, now no one can do these things. If a city is floating in the air thanks to magic, wouldn't it come crashing down? Other forces might be held at bay with magic and now be unleashed. Perhaps horrible creatures have been bound in a supernatural prison and will be let loose, with no one able to truly protect themselves. Are these metaphorical hounds being let loose the harbingers of the end time?

It's fun deciding how the gods are going to destroy everyone. A single blast from an asteroid is brutal but maybe less entertaining than letting something akin to demons have their way with the evil people, while angel-like beings spare the good. Abandoning the species instead could result in a new world order where technology emerges, dovetailing into a creation myth.

Some people are so devout that they'll remain a true believer (in redemption or any other part of the myth) even as the end of time causes the world to crumble around them. Rather than resisting the destruction, they may welcome it and the new world to follow. This could be quite disappointing when they turn out to have been wrong (if so).

ANALOGUES

On Earth, some myths are tightly focused on Judaism, Islam and Christianity, regarding the one God and Christ, so that if we use them, people may realize this. This includes the second coming of a messiah, resurrection for the good, and damnation of the evil. The trick to using these is to decouple them. Worthy people being resurrected is a good idea, but when paired with a messiah, for example, the origins of our end of time myth become too obvious. It's arguably better to cherry pick from existing mythologies than to use ideas wholesale.

Other myths have focused on a cyclic pattern, with decay (moral, spiritual, or physical) eventually leading to salvation and a rebirth into a new reality. The decay could be an alteration in the sun's cycle, a geological upheaval in the planet, or an asteroid strike; all of these alter life as people know it and cause a new reality. A moral decay can lead the gods to decide the species have gone too far to be saved except by wiping out the evil ones and starting anew with the righteous, which could work well in a dystopian setting.

OTHER STORIES

We can also mirror Earth mythologies of gods doing things to each other and mortals. This includes playing tricks, seducing or falling in love, fathering children, attempting murder, and overthrowing the power structure. Anything we mere mortals do is fair game, and myths are often cautionary tales designed to warn a species against certain behaviors. The myths instruct us and our children how to behave. But on our world, many of these stories will have some truth to them because the gods are real. When inventing each myth, determine what's true about it and what isn't. After inventing the story, revisit it, imagining other options and keeping one a secret to reveal later.

Gods have possessions, like anyone. We can create myths where an item fell into mortal hands through theft, misplacement, or even gambling, and caused havoc, possibly resulting in a physical place where strange things happen. This is a great way to invent areas of interest; I've devoted a chapter to it in *Creating Places (The Art of World Building, #2*, "Creating Places of Interest"). Our characters can recover these items, often not on purpose or even realizing it at first. What happens when the god learns someone has it?

CHARACTERISTICS

ALIGNMENT

Anyone who's played role playing games is familiar with the concept of alignment, or good vs. evil. This oversimplified way of viewing gods helps classify, organize, and balance them so we don't have too many evil ones, for example. A degree of balance is preferred unless our story requires an imbalance.

We've seen "neutral," but what does this mean? Neither good nor evil? Or does it mean a pacifist position of non-interference in the machinations of gods or species? Such pacifism is less interesting, but it can create resentment among species who call upon a god who won't answer their prayers, possibly resulting in atheists. By contrast, does a neutral god intervene to stop aggressors from upsetting the balance of good and evil? This can be the attitude of species, too, not just gods.

While "good" and "evil" are widely accepted, the words appeal to younger fans. A more sophisticated audience might appreciate other words that mean the same thing without seeming immature. Some options are "benevolent," "kinder," or "helpful" instead of "good," and "nefarious," "sinister," or "feared" instead of "evil." Readers will get the point without feeling like they're being talked down to.

Those we consider blatantly evil, like Adolf Hitler, likely didn't view themselves that way. Our evil gods might bristle at such a distinction and smite anyone who says such a thing—an act which suggests they are indeed evil. Like us, these deities may rationalize the worldview that gets them called that. A god of domination might believe others need to be ruled, justifying abuses of tyranny, but a god of hate likely can't justify their outlook and might accept being called evil. Giving some thought to this can make our deities more interesting and lead to stories and myths about their interactions.

IDENTIFIERS

Aside from naming our gods, there are other ways to identify them.

TITLES

Deities have titles like "God of War," "Lord of Despair," or "The Weeping God." They can have multiple titles or nicknames, particularly if they oversee more than one area of life. In stories, use only one title at a time to avoid an info dump. One story can reveal one title, another story a different one. We can invent these when needed, skipping this during world building, but always remember to take something invented in a tale and add it to your file on that subject.

PATRONAGE

Gods are sometimes the patron of activities. These can be professions like hunters, farmers, or blacksmiths, or something more general like lovers or children. Who the god patronizes is revealing of their outlook. Look at your god's attributes to decide who they would patronize and who would be praying to them the most. There can be different levels of patronage, such as a god of war favoring all warriors but bestowing greater favors on knights.

SYMBOLS

Symbols are useful for storytelling and gaming. They can be emblazoned on armor, buildings, ships, space stations, and uniforms, or worn as talismans, even branded into flesh. Each scenario tells the audience, and even other characters, something about location or people, allowing easy characterization. Keep symbols, such as a whip suggesting a god of torture, easy to describe in under one sentence. They are usually fairly obvious because residents aren't trying to be creative like us and those with no artistic ability need to draw them. This helps us avoid exposition.

APPEARANCE

We can decide that gods have the ability to choose what form they appear in. On Earth, God is sometimes an old man with a long beard and white robe, maybe sandals, but has been portrayed in recent films as female. Do your gods have typical genders they appear as? Do they appear as human or another species? Or do they have an animal form, or even a monstrous one? Make a general decision about all of them and then decide how each one typically manifests. Appearance can help with creating symbols and nicknames like "The Dragon God" for one who takes that form.

OTHER TRAITS

Gods can be identified by other means. The four elements of air, earth, fire, and water can be associated with four gods, each deity only concerned with one element. Or every god in the pantheon can have one or more elements with which they affiliate. A goddess of love might rule fire, but then so might the goddess of hate. In that example, passion has been used to correlate the deities to the element. A simple justification helps our decisions appeal to an audience; the more obvious it is, the less need for exposition, at the risk of being less creative about it. As with symbols, the world's residents need a straightforward association, not something elaborate.

The seasons can be used in a similar manner. If the gods of love and hate are fire gods because of passion, then this affiliation with heat might also make them summer deities. Or one god can be the only summer deity. Cruelty is considered cold, and so this god might be a winter god, and one of ice (i.e., water). A god of agriculture is clearly a god of the earth and either spring (planting) or autumn (the harvest). A goddess of birth can be associated with spring planting.

The seven colors in the spectrum can also be associated with these deities and subsequently, their symbols and the colors favored by their followers. If your goddess of love favors orange or yellow (going with the fire motif), then perhaps her priests' robes are the same colors. A god of death and/or fear will likely favor black; if we want a less predictable color, we can rationalize that death is not an evil but something natural that happens to everyone.

BEHAVIOR

A god who never does anything might as well not exist from a world building standpoint. For your pantheon, decide what is considered acceptable and unacceptable behavior and whether the gods generally obey this. Each deity will have a different viewpoint, with some being very lawful, others agreeing but not overly caring, some chafing but agreeing, and others outright disdainful and either openly thwarting such rules or doing so secretly, possibly while being amused that they're doing so. We'll need to know our gods to make these decisions.

Do gods punish offending deities? Do guilty gods submit to the punishment (respecting the law they've broken) or resist, possibly by fleeing? We might decide that there's a prison for deities and what its properties are and what, if anything, is preventing other gods, or their followers, from doing a prison break.

How do gods punish their species? Death, a nasty afterlife, misfortune, or removing talent, like one for magic? And for what offenses? Swearing with a god's name is a good one except that so many people might be doing this that the gods would be awfully busy. Failure to undertake a promised mission makes sense for adventurers. Not defending a temple is another. Destroying one is even better.

These more serious offenses are more likely to attract divine punishment. Myths about famous people who've suffered a given fate serve as cautionary tales that can be mentioned to spice up our narratives.

REPUTATION

Some gods and their followers have a reputation that immediately comes to mind if they're mentioned. A god of cruelty might force self-mutilation on its priests. For a god of love, this might be orgies. A god of wrath might be prone to outbursts of anger, making people afraid to even say his name. Does anyone demand sacrifice? Decide how people think of each of your gods (positive/negative) and why that is. Whether or not the god obeys godly rules will come into play. This is where myths can help shape their reputation, too. For some deities, this will be easier than others.

INTERACTION

Do your gods ever visit the world and peoples they created? Why, how often, and for what? Do they have to be summoned or can they appear wherever they want? Are there restrictions on where they can go? Only other gods are likely to have created a restriction powerful enough that another god must obey. Are there time limits on how long a god can remain here? These limits should have a rationale because we assume gods are without limits.

World builders sometimes decide that the gods will not directly influence events; it's too convenient to have them swoop in and fix things or cause issues when our characters are doing well. One way to avoid this is having the god's behavior be that which caused the story. Past events can also have set something in motion, and this is where myths come into play, with our characters discovering the details or truth of a legend, maybe the hard way.

CREATIONS

Gods are assumed to have invented the world and its life, whether by accident or on purpose. We don't need to give a reason for this, but our world building can be better if we do. We can take some reasons that we have for our own creative work and attribute it to gods, such as a love of doing so. We're curious how our children will turn out while guiding and shaping the result, so the gods can, too.

We can decide which god(s) created what life forms. This really means cherry-picking ones to make decisions about, since no one cares which god invented tomatoes, for example. On the other hand, a plant that devours species might be improved by deciding an evil god invented it, especially if it only eats certain species—namely the ones that god doesn't like.

While a god of war is an obvious choice for the one who invented a weapon, even a god of love could do so if it's reminiscent of Cupid's bow. Look at your god's trait list and imagine what items they might possess for themselves or have given to the world. Decide if there's a limit on what can be created; maybe plants and animals are okay, but the gods must agree to invent a humanoid species. Our god of chaos might be forbidden from creating anything but do it anyway, resulting in some unpredictable monster.

PLACES

Our gods can create special places, which are typically supernatural. These can be on the world, between worlds, or an alternate reality. Prisons, meeting places, means of travel, and hiding places are some possibilities. Explanations are typically better but not needed, as inhabitants often won't know the truth; it's unlikely they'll even learn of these locations, but our characters will or there's no point inventing them.

Temples, whether abandoned or not, are places where gods are likely to visit, and sometimes their religion will build these up extensively. Can the gods be reached here? Is there anything special about the place where they appear? What about the altar where sacrifices to sinister gods were made? Is a church the way to enter a portal to where that god dwells?

The afterlife is a unique place that will be covered in *Cultures and Beyond (The Art of World Building, #3)*.

WHERE TO START

We can create gods by making a list of things we'd like gods of, like love. We can also reimagine existing Earth gods. Both options are delved into below.

STARTING WITH ATTRIBUTES

With a pantheon, each god has areas they oversee, like love or war, which are seldom assigned to more than one god; there's only one god of love. Each deity can be the god of more than one thing, and these lesser concerns are typically related as if one is an outgrowth of another. A god of love might also be the god of marriage and family. The god of cunning might be the god of war, manipulation, bribery, strategy, and deceit. These additional traits can help us understand our god more than assigning a lone trait. Grouping attributes also helps us create fewer gods. Different people will group things differently, which is good. There are no right or wrong answers.

Make a master list of traits and begin grouping them. You'll start realizing who this individual is—personality, interests, and temperament. Traits you overlooked can be added to the master list or an individual god's. Sometimes a trait might fit more than one god, but that's okay as long as it's not a primary trait, like love.

STARTING WITH ANALOGUES

We can model deities from Earth pantheons or another author, though this dips perilously close to plagiarism and should be done carefully. Research the gods of a culture and make an attribute list this way. Take note of how the deity is viewed, what they're the god of, and their relationships with other ones. When you have a dozen or more gods written down, you can see all the ideas you like in one place. Make another list that will become *your* deities deity and start raiding the first list, combining attributes into new gods.

For example, Zeus is the leader and father figure to other Greek gods and throws lightning bolts. Most of us would recognize that if you did it verbatim, but you can change his appearance and weapon to something else. Zeus also fathered children with human women (as have other Greek gods). Assign that habit to another god instead. By mixing and matching ideas, you create something unique. Invent a god of storms and have him be the lightning bolt thrower.

3

CREATING A SPECIES

Creating a species is one of the most rewarding but challenging aspects of world building. This chapter focuses on ensuring your species is close to the competition (such as elves and dwarves) in quality and depth. We can feel daunted by all that we could invent, but remember that we can always ditch things that aren't working. Having fun with it and taking it one subject at a time go a long way toward keeping it fun.

Appendix 2 is a template for creating a species. It includes more comments and advice. An editable file can be downloaded for free by signing up for the newsletter at http://www.artofworldbuilding.com/newsletter/

SPECIES OR RACE?

Terminology affects perception and our ability to organize our creations. Fantasy readers are familiar with "race" denoting the difference between an elf and dwarf, for example. These races are very different in physical features, temperament, and society. They seem totally unrelated except for being humanoid. By contrast, on Earth, we only have humans, a species, and use the word race to distinguish between different biological variations of us. This section explores the difference between "race" and "species" and when we should use each term in our setting, though there's no right or wrong answer.

THE TERMS

What's a race? The answer can be complicated, but on Earth, race has been described as nothing more than a social construct to describe different versions of Homo sapiens (i.e., humans), who are 99.9% the same, having no genetic differences to warrant classification (into races or anything else). In other words, genetics has nothing to do with the term race and more to do with the word species. This means that if two humanoids are genetically different, they'll be considered separate species.

Separate DNA = different species.

Shared DNA = races of a species.

In SF, humanoids originating on different planets will have different genes, so calling them species makes more sense. In fantasy, humanoids are most often from the same world; it's possible for them to share genes and therefore be races of one species. Since elves, dwarves, and others are invented, no genetic material exists to determine if they are, in fact, genetically different. One could assume that the pointed ears of elves must mean there's a genetic difference, but this is superficial. On Earth, human races have different eye shapes, noses, and more while still being genetically the same. Fantasy humanoids could indeed be races, sharing DNA.

Small people, also known as dwarves, exist on Earth, but their distinctive height and other characteristics are caused by a medical or genetic disorder, which is only sometimes passed down from parents (due to genes). It is not a definite outcome, but in fantasy worlds, a dwarf is a different race with a guaranteed passing down of their different genes to children, which suggest they are really a species. We wouldn't expect a fantasy dwarf to give birth to a human, but Earth dwarves have done exactly that.

In some books, authors will say that elves, dwarves, and humans all derive from the same ancestry (same DNA) and they are therefore races, which seems a good term. On the other hand, if we say that the gods created elves, dwarves, and humans separately and that these beings didn't divide themselves during evolution, they probably aren't races. They are different species. Our audience may be indifferent to this and exposition to explain it will bog down our story. They will expect "race" and might balk at "species," so consider this, too.

If our gods are capable of creating one species, why haven't they created two or more? Did some event stop them and they never got around to it? They just did one and let it separate into races on its own? Or did the gods cause those races to develop? Are the gods taking a hands-off approach to the world and not interfering beyond inventing this one species? If they're involved in everyday life, why not create more species?

If races don't exist on a biological level, species is the other obvious term to use, but even biologists struggle with what is known as the "species problem." There are over two dozen definitions of the word "species." If scientists can't define it, how can we? The word is just used to group similar organisms and is what the average person thinks of when considering a cat vs. a dog, for example. Both races and species can interbreed, producing offspring, rendering the distinction between them a moot point, so this shouldn't figure in our thinking.

BIO-DIVERSITY

To make a decision, consider how diverse your creations are. If they're all humanoid, it suggests shared DNA and they are races. Elves, dwarves, hobbits, orcs, humans, and other fantasy tropes have two arms and legs, one head, and no tail, etc. But if we create one with wings, another with gills and other adaptations for the water, and another with four legs, these suggest different species. Wouldn't a dragon be a different species from Homo sapiens?

On Earth, we distinguish between Caucasians, Asians, and more with the word "race." If such races exist on our world, we should also call them race. But if we also have elves and dwarves and call those races, too, isn't that confusing? Wouldn't humans, elves, and dwarves be species, and Caucasians, Asians, and blacks be races of humans? High elves and drow would be races of elves. This makes more sense than saying they are races of some unnamed parent humanoid species.

A HIERARCHY

A hierarchy can illustrate the problems of using race and species poorly. Consider this list where everyone is lumped together as races:

1. Daekais
2. Kadeans
3. Humans
4. Mandeans
5. Morkais
6. Nideans

Can you tell which ones are related? If so, it's only from my naming convention; two of them have "kais" in their name and three of them have "deans" in theirs. This lack of structure results from seeing everything as a race of one species despite their differences. As it turns out, two of those humanoids have wings, and three of the others live in water, having gills and other adaptations. Doesn't the below make more sense?

1. Humans
2. Kais
   a. Daekais
   b. Morkais
3. Mandeans
   a. Kadeans
   b. Nideans

Numbers one, two, and three are species. The differences between them are enough that no one would confuse one for another. Letters a and b are races under their respective species. I refer to daekais as a race of kais, not just a generic "race" of…unspecified. If I want to refer to daekais and morkais simultaneously, I can use "kais" to do so.

Let's take a look at some traditional fantasy races. Ask yourself which is better among these organizations:

1. Drow
2. Humans
3. Hill dwarves
4. Mountain dwarves
5. Wood elves

Or this:

1. Dwarves
   a. Hill dwarves
   b. Mountain dwarves
2. Elves
   a. Drow
   b. Wood elves
3. Humans

You may have little reason to point out such distinctions to your audience; a paragraph of explanation is not advised. Using "species" has an added benefit of pulling readers out of their comfort zone of expectations. Some who feel strongly one way or another will tell you otherwise, but it's your world and you are its ultimate god.

SHOULD WE CREATE A SPECIES?

In SF, we may need to create new species, but in fantasy we have the option not to. This section helps you decide on whether to do it or not.

IN SCIENCE FICTION

Aside from little green aliens, inventors of SF have no public domain species available. We can't use Vulcans from *Star Trek* or Na'-vi from *Avatar* because someone else owns them. We either have only humans or must invent humanoid (or not) species. Do you want your planet-hopping characters to encounter unique lifeforms on different planets or on other spacecraft? That and aliens arriving on Earth are the only scenario where we must create them, as there are plenty of SF stories with only humans, especially those involving explorers from Earth.

In a universe like *Star Trek*, some species are ever-present while others are episodic, only appearing in one or two shows. The latter need far less development time. It might be wise to create a few well-developed species (who are part of a crew we use repeatedly) but then spend less effort on everything else. Some ideas might have limited use anyway; rather than discard them, use them for one story and move on. Riskier ideas are well-suited to this because if our audience doesn't like them, we're not revisiting them anyway.

A caveat here is that the opposite could happen: we might find ourselves using them more than initially intended, in which case we must be careful not to box ourselves into a corner. Don't make unnecessary comments in early uses of them, such as, "They never leave their planet." Unless that's part of that story, this restriction could come back to haunt us when we want them traveling. There are ways around that, like deciding they've been driven from the world, but you get the idea. A side-effect of thinly developed ideas is accidental conflict when we decide to more fully develop them *after* publishing them.

IN FANTASY

Fantasy species are well defined, popular, and mostly public domain. No one can stop us from using them, which is one reason why seemingly everyone does. Does this make them over-used? Are people clamoring for something they haven't seen? Are you? If so, you could skip to the next section, "Creating a Species," right now, but there are a few other points to consider.

Is it okay to present the usual species but with minor or significant changes and still call them the same thing? For minor variations, yes (see "What's In a Name?" in Chapter 1). For more significant alterations, we might want to just strike out farther on purpose and add a new name. Once freed from the original concept via a name, it becomes easier to reimagine an elf or dwarf. Remember the rule of three when using an analogue: at least three changes so people are less likely to realize it's a modified elf.

Sometimes it seems like we can read ten books by ten different authors and get ten slightly different versions of an elf. Is that good or bad? They're on different planets, after all, and might develop differently, but it begs the question of why the humans are usually the same as those on Earth. And the horses. And plants.

There is an important caveat to species that aren't public domain, like Ents and Hobbits from *The Lord of the*

Rings. We can create a very similar species and then give them a different name. The treants and halflings from *Dungeons and Dragons* come to mind. This has been done for legal reasons, as the original species belong to their creator, Tolkien. We run the risk of legal trouble with this anyway and it goes against the idea of creating something new, but the option remains. It is arguably best to put our own spin on an analogue while renaming it; with enough changes, audiences won't immediately think of a known species.

CREATING SOMETHING DIFFERENT

Inventing unique species can help our work stand out (hopefully in a good way) and even invigorate love of the genre for both us and our audience. With so many people using public domain species, there's probably little we can say about them that hasn't been said before. How many authors have used the long lives of elves to comment on how impatient humans can be? There are constraints on us from these species, possibly making us long for our freedom. But there's also safety there, in the comfort of familiarity, and an assurance that if our audience doesn't like our work, the species won't be their reason. There's risk to invention, but reward, too.

If our species will be alongside public domain ones in our work, comparisons are inevitable. Doing a good job is even more important. The standard species are high quality and set a high bar for us. This chapter is designed to help us get over it.

HOW OFTEN THE SETTING WILL BE USED

It doesn't make sense to spend many hours developing a species for a short story. We'll never have a chance to reveal much of our work. If we'd like to develop a detailed species anyway, then we should invent for a setting we'll use repeatedly across multiple works. Creating a thinly developed species for shorter works on a single-use world is another good approach, which can work especially well if the species is bizarre and might face resistance from an audience.

We might invent a species to tell a specific story, which allows us to tailor our invention to our use. This keeps down unwanted or unneeded invention but might also restrict us, when freedom is one reason we're creating species. Conversely, we might invent a species first and begin to think of story ideas or ways we can use it. This latter approach might yield more material than intended, but having ideas is never a bad thing. We can end up with multiple stories while retaining the freedom to invent. Regardless of our approach, we shouldn't feel that building a species is a waste of time because it can take our work to unexpected and great places. Everyone benefits.

SCOPE

How much effort to expend on creating a species will depend on intentions, but there's a range of possibility from extreme world building to hardly any.

THE MINIMUM

At the least, we must decide on physical appearance and an overall disposition that's shared across members of a species. Such life forms are often used as little more than a beast for characters to overcome in their quests. Ogres, orcs, and other henchmen types from fantasy are good examples. They seldom talk or do much more than get killed by the heroes. A more benevolent species can also have limited use, like Chewbacca from *Star Wars*.

He's a Wookiee, but in the original three films, we never see another Wookiee (George Lucas may have added more in the background when he altered the films later). That we only saw one Wookiee made Chewbacca synonymous with his species. We had no Wookiees to compare him to and his personality traits might as well have been the traits of all of them. That he never spoke a word we could understand eliminated cultural, societal, and other issues that minimized the effort needed to create him. He is useful primarily as a constant physical companion who can fight and do things while Han Solo has conversations without the distraction of doing Chewbacca's tasks.

It is Harrison Ford's acting talents that make Chewy work as a character; his funny responses to Chewy's nonsensical growls are what really characterize the Wookiee. The same can be said of C-3PO's responses to the unintelligible R2-D2. Despite all of this, Chewbacca works, but this approach arguably succeeds onscreen better than on paper, due to the inflections, body language, and tone used by actors. In books, a character or species with such limited use is hard to make memorable; our readers may forget the character is there or wonder what they're for. The character is little more than a henchman, albeit a positive one.

As a side note, Wookiee is capitalized for some reason but your species or races should not be; that's not a title or proper name. You never see "human" capitalized unless it's the start of a sentence. One justification for capitalizing it is when the name is synonymous with a region. For example, Germans are from Germany so we capitalize it. Wookiees are from Kashyyyk so this rule doesn't appear to apply, which just shows you we can get away with things like this.

Continuing with *Star Wars* as an example, there are countless other species shown but never named. They are extras on the set, many with compelling appearances, and that is all we experience of them. This works better onscreen than on paper; a picture really is worth a thousand words, which we don't want to waste on a multitude of characters who have minimal impact on our story.

THE MAXIMUM

At the other extreme is a fully-developed species, including their habitat, climate, settlement preferences, appearance of head, body, and clothing, their gods, society, languages, customs, history, relationships with other species, supernatural and technology talents and attitudes, and combat skills. It can be easy to go overboard inventing things we might never use, but it can also make a great impression of depth and believability.

A major issue with this is not only hours but months, even years of refinement, weeding out the lesser aspects that don't stand the test of time while rounding out and improving the good ideas. As with most things, world building skill grows with practice, making this culling part of the process; this book is designed to give you a head start. As we go on to invent sovereign powers, monsters, animals and plants, we'll continuously update our species, integrating everything and improving realism.

IN MODERATION

If done right, splitting the difference can be a sensible choice. The next section and species template (in the appendix) can help you can make an informed decision about which areas to work on. I recommend deciding on habitat, whether the species lives in joint settlements, overall disposition, appearance, and their relationships with each other and your other creations. Areas to skimp for now can be clothing, gods, characteristics (like agility, intelligence, and morale), language, customs, history, combat, and details on their supernatural and technological level.

"Skimping" ranges from overlooking a subject altogether to jotting down a few words about it. You'll have to decide what is skimped based on your needs, but it's worth it to think about every subject to see if you have any concepts. Sometimes ideas beget ideas, meaning that the act of writing down one subject causes you to think of other details. This happens more often as you develop other aspects of a world, resulting in an integrated setting that could stand out in the crowded marketplace.

HABITAT

Environment is crucial to how a humanoid species develops, just like plants and animals. This may not appear true with humans because it's been eons since we evolved into what we are and we don't remember back that far. We'll also live anywhere, making it seem like habitat has no impact. Our only apparent adaptation is to the sun, changing our skin color near the tropics. If locale affects our invented species, that may depend on how extreme that habitat is and whether they ever leave.

Environment strongly affects a water dwelling species, possibly causing gills, webbed fingers and toes, or making them amphibious. They may have teeth and claws for spearing or holding fish. Their clothes and weapons will be different. Plate mail would likely sink them. Onshore, they might use slings but not bows (the former is less damaged by water, easier to carry beneath the waves, and ammunition might abound near shore). Maybe they take the poisonous spines from fish and use them as blow darts. They probably have less contact with other species that aren't underwater all the time (or ever). Maybe they closely watch ships, attacking them or rescuing those from sinking ships at battle sites. They could be part of the crew. Do they go on land, and how often?

A species that spends most of its time underground will also be affected. They will have much better sight in low light conditions, as there's little or no natural light, except for possible bioluminescence, which could include them. They're probably shorter; this might be a cliché from dwarves, but if you had to tunnel through rock, you wouldn't want to make passages bigger than needed.

Having to do this over millennia will influence height downward. An underground species might be less than ideally nourished, becoming shorter in generations. Where are they getting their food? This likely forces them outside and into dealing with other species.

In fantasy, a common trope is for elves to only live in forests. Has this habitat affected them physically? They don't have tails for climbing trees or even strong hands with claws for grasping bark while climbing. They either live on the ground like humans or up in trees so big that they don't need climbing skills, having built stairs, bridges, and whole buildings up there. They're often said to be thin; is that so that can hide behind a tree more easily? The only impact appears to be on their attachment to the woodland plants and animals, which affects personality and culture, but arguably not their bodies.

The idea of elves in a forest and dwarves in a mountain, seldom leaving, is pervasive in fantasy, but is it realistic? Usually the elves are given a haughtiness or contempt for humans (who are everywhere) to explain why they keep to themselves so much. Dwarves are paranoid, distrustful or grumpy and anti-social.

If we're going to create new species, would they be more useful if they not only have a preferred habitat, but are willing to travel and create new settlements elsewhere, or at least be a significant part of them? If so, then we have two choices: they've always been travelers and therefore habitat had no more effect on them than it does on humans, or they kept to their habitat for millennia, long enough to affect their bodies, before venturing into the world more.

In the latter case, what initially drove them out? War? Famine? A slow realization that other species have things to offer and trade? The arrival of settlers from far away? Protection of their assets? Habitat and history are comingled. The inciting incident can be decided later.

ISOLATED SETTLEMENTS

Creating Places (The Art of World Building, #2) covers creating actual settlements, but at a high level, consider what cities created by our new species, and only by them, are like. These are traits most of the towns will share. If the species is short, buildings will reflect this, unless they're welcoming of visitors from other species, in which case they may have some places designated for taller species.

Consider the possible materials that your species builds with; stone, wood, natural cliffs and caves, or a conglomeration of everything. Are they good builders? That implies some sophistication and engineering skills, but if this is a barbaric, violent, uneducated species, they're likely nomadic or living in abandoned, ruined, or conquered settlements built by others. A benevolent and educated species will likely have towering monuments of stone and glass. In SF, the differing technological levels will have a huge impact on not only settlements but warfare, travel, and culture, with those who lack the ability to create advanced things having to steal them from others (or destroy them) to level the playing field.

What influence have outside events and life caused on the settlement? Is your species peaceful but has learned the value of a wall, moats, and anti-siege engines? How fortified are your species' cities and why? Are there nearby threats of violence? Or are they paranoid that others want what they have, like access to a mountain and its gems, metals, and minerals? Has the forest been cleared around their settlement so an advancing army cannot benefit from its cover? How would that work if the species adores woodland?

Why do they prefer to remain aloof? Have they been at war with others in their area for too long? Are they doing something secret? Did a plague wipe out many of them and now this is how they live generations later? Fear is a powerful motivation. Do they have contempt for the character of other species the way elves are often depicted having contempt for humanity? Is the issue cultural? What's the cost of their isolation? Lack of support in wars with other enemies? Lack of access to resources someone else might control? Or are they the ones depriving others of access to something? And why? All of this figures into the cultural and societal decisions we'll make.

We may decide that our species has isolated settlements in some areas of the world but is more integrated in others, in which case the sort of local events mentioned above are probably behind the differences. There are many more varieties than the seeming de facto isolation common in fantasy.

JOINT SETTLEMENTS

Enter the joint settlement, one created by multiple species together.

Have you noticed the tendency for all cities to be built by humans for humans? The likely cause is human authors writing for a human audience, featuring mostly human main characters. Other species might live there, but it's mostly a human place. Maybe a species has a quarter, like the French Quarter in New Orleans, but that's about it. Perhaps it's more realistic that a settlement starts off as a village built by one species, but as time passes, a nearby species becomes welcome as visitors, merchants, and allies. As the village becomes a town and then city, isn't it likely that more than one species is involved in calling it home, with all the rights that this entails? Sure, there'd be growing pains as two species with different outlooks clash, but it will become a joint settlement sooner or later.

There can be resistance on the part of those who founded it, but that's a good source of tension and history, making your world richer. When we add more than three species, it becomes harder (in time) for one to be miffed that the community used to be just theirs. It becomes a true melting pot. We can gain inspiration here from the cultural strain in the United States between the Europeans who founded the country and minorities or immigrants. This works on a smaller scale like settlements. In SF, visiting aliens may have also influenced the settlement, whether socially, intellectually, or with physical accommodations.

How likely is it that humans are the only ones who've built a city outside of forests and mountains? If we have a bunch of species that are reasonably cooperative, not likely. Animosities can exist and even be more pronounced from sharing a settlement more equally. This can be more interesting than everyone sulking in their preferred habitat and shunning everyone else. This integration is something to revisit as we create multiple cities; when working on maps, which is covered in *Creating Places (The Art of World Building, #2)*, think about which species are in which land features and who is residing in any settlement you draw on the map.

TERRAIN

We've already thought about underground or under-water environments, but what about those on land? The anatomy of a species will impact their terrain preferences. Something that doesn't run well or use horses might not like open land because pursuit and fleeing are both more troublesome; perhaps they've developed an adaptation, like being able to camouflage skin to hide instead. Skin coloring might be greens and browns in a forest setting.

Something with wings likely prefers living in mountains, both because anything that can't fly will have a harder time reaching them and so it's easier to take flight. They could live along forest edges, depending on how big they and the trees are. If they've built cities, towers will dominate, many having open roofs. They're unlikely to live on plains. A desert offers little when they can just go somewhere far more habitable with little trouble.

Their bodies might not be the reason a terrain is preferred, but their lifestyle. A species that enjoys stalking, killing, and consuming other species might prefer woodland for all the opportunity to hide. If the species is smaller and four-legged, plains might be good, too, as tall grass allows hiding (think of lions). A species that excels at jumping and climbing might prefer mountainous terrain, especially if they have great endurance and don't easily tire with the additional exertion; conversely, a species without endurance may avoid mountains or open land (an inability to run for a long time means they get caught by something that can) and prefer forests, for hiding.

CLIMATE

Humans will live anywhere, but what about your species? A water-dwelling one will be influenced by ocean currents, possibly migrating and having more than one settlement. If a land-based species doesn't build settlements, they're outside a lot and likely prefer temperate to warm climates, being found farther from the equator less often. An underground species likely couldn't care less about climate, which doesn't affect them except their crops and livestock; as a result, they might dominate cold regions.

In SF, with interplanetary travel, the shipboard environment will be suited to one species' preferred climate, affecting temperature, humidity, and the brightness and even color of light. Another species might find traveling on such a ship uncomfortable. What if our ship has multiple species working together and some can't handle heat or cold? Might there be areas where they can go to warm up or cool down? Maybe they wear clothing designed to insulate or cool them. Such suits would be needed anyway if landing on a world or in a climate they deem inhospitable, solving the issue but still giving us a detail to comment on. Suit malfunctions raise another issue.

DISPOSITION

Is our species good, evil, or more complicated? Our intended use of them will help in subsequent decisions.

Something violent, uncivilized, and uneducated may not be welcomed in society. Maybe the idea of them is used to frighten children into behaving. They're a danger for travelers, especially non-warriors. Characters might have relatives injured, killed, or even eaten by this species. People go missing, in the wilderness or in space, whether there's a gruesome crime scene or no sign of the body. Its presence causes caravans to be armed and scouting patrols to be around the community's borders. Settlement or space station defenses will take their abilities into consideration when arranging armed forces. Weapons might be designed with them in mind. People can be skilled in tracking and scouting for them. The species will have a reputation that affects the lives of those they threaten.

A pleasant, communicative, and benevolent species will be welcomed by other societies, though possibly with reservations. They could be bringing supplies only they have access to, like plants, gems, or special weapons and armor of their creation. They may exchange information on recent activities by obnoxious species. Our characters might have friends in that species, who could've saved, trained, or befriended a relative. Maybe people aspire to be like them.

The caveat here is the human model—we can't be predicted to be nefarious or benevolent as a whole. Some like to believe mankind is basically good, and while not getting all philosophical about it, this obviously doesn't mean we don't do horrible things to each other and even animals, plants, and the Earth. Is our new species more predictable than us or equally complex?

If they have a uniform disposition, is there a reason for this? Did a set of gods with the same disposition create them? If evil gods created ogres, maybe that explains their attitude. Were they the result of an accident that influenced them? Did they result from breeding sentient life with animals or monsters? Did someone evil or good create them and use magic or something else to ensure their disposition? How strong is that disposition? If they were created ten thousand years ago and something situational at the time made them evil, hasn't that situation likely passed and maybe now they're different, less extreme? Or is it perpetual and they're even more upset?

An evil species might be less useful if shunned by society, effectively relegating them to a smarter monster out in the woods. This places creative limits on us that might be undesirable, particularly if we intend to use our setting for many stories. That species can't do things inside a city without sneaking in, for example, but how many times do we want to use them that way before they become a predictable caricature of themselves? This can be solved by creating two races of similar appearance but with opposing dispositions, such as elves and drow (dark elves).

This can greatly extend the reach of a uniformly good or evil species, allowing new uses for them. It also creates a problem for those on our world: does the person we're looking at belong to the good one or the evil one? Can the person standing before them be trusted? Using elves and drow as an example, the first all good, the second all evil, elves would be trusted, but now people know that drow exist. A drow could pretend to be an elf to gain access to somewhere or something. An elf could pretend to be a drow to infiltrate somewhere under drow control. If you like this idea but also like races that can be physically distinguished from others in the species, just create additional races: one that looks different and one that doesn't; for example, elves and drow looking the same, and a third kind of elf that looks different from both.

APPEARANCE

When creating a species, start with physical characteristics; bodies influence the minds that develop. Like it or not, appearance plays a crucial role in life, even if no one's likely to draw our species or otherwise see it. The overall impression and details combine to add characterization opportunities that shouldn't be overlooked. It's okay to start with envisioning a specific character, but try to get a sense of how the species generally looks, too. This allows us to not only define them all, but then comment on how our character matches or defies expectations, without which, our audience has a limited understanding of how this person fits in (or not) with their own kind or others.

For example, if your species is generally slovenly but this character is neat, maybe he gets more respect from other species. And what does it say about him? Do his kind find him arrogant? Does he care? Why is he like this? Does he aspire to be better? Or does he dress neatly to keep people from suspecting his character is bad? Does this provide him better opportunities?

A neat species but a sloppy character can have the opposite effect. Maybe his own kind think he's a slob in personal and work habits, but other species find him more down to earth. Maybe he's a gambler and wants to fit in with lowlife friends. Or he's disguising himself like an undercover cop. Is he so consumed by his work that he doesn't pay attention to his appearance (a cliché)? He's just clueless or indifferent to the consequences?

ARE THEY HUMANOID?

There's a tendency to create humanoid species like elves and dwarves instead of spider-like ones, for example. This is preferred for most species because otherwise things might get too weird for our audience, or too much like a cartoon. While there's always room for these, non-humanoids have their challenges.

With humanoids, we don't have to decide what they eat, how often they sleep, and other biological basics. They mingle well with humans, being able to live in similar buildings, use horses, and need fewer unusual physical things. By contrast, would a giant spider sleep in a bed, or eat with utensils, or consume the same food? How would one travel if not on foot? Such considerations might be needed if we go this route. It could make things more interesting for both us and the audience.

With a non-humanoid, our ability to quickly and skillfully describe them matters because readers have to imagine them, unless we're in a visual medium. While it's great to have explanations for anatomical features, audiences are used to bizarre things without getting one iota of explanation. Be forewarned that such creations have a tendency to be monsters, or viewed as one, a subject discussed more in Chapter 5, "Creating Monsters."

HEAD

When creating a head, think about every last facial feature, as described next, but when describing a species to an audience, it's often best to comment on the most important features rather than overwhelm with detail. It's even better to do so while describing a character's mood at the moment, as evidenced by the effect of that mood on those features.

HUMANOIDS

Below are some features to write about and the options that are easiest to describe with a word that most will recognize; if we have to explain a facial feature too much, maybe it's better to just go with something easier to envision and convey. An example of this problem is the word "monolid," (listed below in text about eyes) because while we've all seen this, we've likely never heard the word.

Other names can be used in our files but not in our writing because they're of Earth origin, like "Roman nose" or "Cupid's bow," unless Earth figures in our work; we'd need another name, but then no one will know what we're talking about and we'll have to describe it. To see images of many features listed, do an internet search.

Feature	Options
Face/jawline	round, oval, square, heart-shaped
Brow	prominent (often caused by deep set eyes) or shallow (monolid)
Eyebrows	rounded, arched (and to what degree), mono brow
Eyes	round, slanted, deep set, up/down turned (at the outside corner), wide/close set, hooded (as if hidden behind overhanging eyelids all the time), protruding (the opposite of hooded), and monolid (the opposite of deep set, where the brow appears less prominent, as in some Asians)
Iris	shape (vertical/horizontal slit, round, cat's eye, crescent) and typical colors
Nose	straight, long and wide (like blacks), hawkish, snub, thin and pointed, bulbous, upturned, aquiline, broad with large nostrils, and the basic large nose
Mouth	average, wide, small, full or thin lips (sometimes each is different), rounded/pointed/absent Cupid's bow
Teeth	straight, crooked, missing, stained, pointed, serrated, poisonous, tiny, large, and multiple rows (like a shark)

Chin	protruding, cleft, thin and pointing, round, square, jutting, receding (i.e., almost no chin), and long (often points forward)

If you can't draw, then your decisions may look different than you intended when someone like an artist you hire assembles them into a face. There are various games, such as Wii, or online tools that allow you to create a character or avatar that looks like you. You can experiment with these face generators to give you a head start on this. A quick Google search for face avatar generators turned up these free, online programs I experimented with:

Pimp the face:
http://www.pimptheface.com/create/

Face your manga:
http://www.faceyourmanga.com/editmangatar.php

The second allowed me to generate some images in a few fun minutes of poking around. While I wouldn't use it in my work, it gives me a good reference image in my files and can be handed to an artist to draw something similar.

NON-HUMANOIDS

The heads of non-humanoids can be based on animals or invented from scratch, but you'll want an understanding of why a feature exists or it might not make sense. In a monster, an explanation isn't necessary; after all, the creepiness of things that don't make sense are part of why it's a monster (the bizarre and nonsensical frightens). The bar is set higher for a species. We needn't ever explain it, but having the species use the feature in a way that makes it clear there's a rationale behind it helps us.

For example, sharks have jaws that can distend for a

wider bite, with rows of replaceable, serrated teeth for ripping meat. If our species also eats something (on land?) raw and with high fat content (like a seal), then it might have this as well. If it eats a different prey, then it won't. A crocodile drowns victims by holding them underwater, so it doesn't need shearing teeth. Also, such teeth wouldn't make sense if our species eats plants or cooks all meals.

Predators tend to have eyes facing forward, while prey tend to have them on the sides to see predators coming more easily (usually from behind). If our species is truly only prey and never predator, consider this option. Prey also tend to have ears that can independently swivel, but a hunter might also have this skill. A wet nose is designed to catch particles for dissolving and smelling, so if we say our species has a great sense of smell but don't say they have a wet nose, that's less believable, though most people won't know that.

BODY

HUMANOIDS

If our species is humanoid, our body design work is largely done. Areas needing description are mostly those of overall size, height, mass, and fitness standards. The prevalence of facial hair on males and average cleanliness of all genders can also characterize them, but these are partly cultural, too, and result from behaviors. A species that does messy work, like farming, might become less careful about cleanliness so that their slovenly appearance characterizes them. Deciding on some bodily issues can come before or after we form an impression of world view.

Females will be different from males in usually minor ways. Human females are more feminine than males (hence the word), but we can reverse this, making the females brutish and the males delicate; this will benefit from a good reason. Do females wear jewelry or otherwise try to appear more attractive to males, or is the species too brutish for that? Is mating like humans or do females go into heat like animals? Is there a mating season? Much of this is cultural.

Standards of beauty have changed in human history, with larger woman having been seen as better bearers of children long ago, but now thinner women are all the rage, so how are the females? Is it the women who pursue the males, who must try to attract them, and if so, what affect does this have on both genders physically? Making a humanoid body different from those of humans (in more than superficial ways) involves thinking about other aspects of their lives.

Size and mass influence not just strength and endurance, but capabilities. A species with hands that are much larger or smaller than humans will have trouble wielding weapons or using tools designed for us. If they aren't sophisticated enough to invent their own, then is someone creating these for them? Do they just steal the items? Or do they capture people with the know-how to make them, then force these slaves to do that work?

Size also affects relationships with enemies and allies. If our species is three feet tall, do they just run away from something over six feet tall, or do they swarm while attacking? Have they developed great endurance from all that running or are they just faster than everything and then good at hiding? Being encumbered by possessions makes running harder, so do they travel light? Does another, taller species protect them? Is there a flying species who knows this running species will drop everything and flee, so they follow along hoping to pick up the discarded items, like carrion birds circling a battlefield? If they're larger than everyone, are they fearless? Is that overconfidence that can be used against them?

In SF in particular, many aliens have skin like reptiles, not only with scales but similar coloring. This should have a biological basis, such as protection from the elements or predators. Making their skin poisonous is another option, which can introduce some cultural issues. They'd need to avoid touching humans, for example, and might be wearing gloves or other gear to protect others.

NON-HUMANOID

If our species is not humanoid, basing it on an animal can help realize its body and avoid something unintentionally silly. Gigantism is an option but is arguably the least interesting because it's a run of the mill creature except for its size. If we also modify our analogue, this is more attractive.

Combining features of animals and humanoids is benefitted by having some understanding why an animal has a feature so we can decide if it makes sense for our species. If our species has a tail, what do they use it for? A weapon is a good answer; that suggests protecting their rear but that they might also be a predator *and* prey. Is the tail is long enough to strike forward? Can that tail sting? How venomous is it? How fast acting is the poison? If it's designed to use against those with weapon skills and not just animals, a poison would be fast acting to neutralize a threat quickly, even if it sedates instead of kills. All of this is true of poisonous teeth and claws.

Research every feature to see why it exists. Why do turtles have shells? Why don't snakes have legs? Tails are often for climbing, but clearly that's not true for a horse. Horns and tusks are used for fighting and even digging in dirt. Coloring may be for camouflage or warning. Wings are obviously for flight, but there are flightless birds, so understand why that happens before inventing one; they typically exist on an island that has no predators, so creating a flightless bird that lives amid many predators doesn't make sense unless it has developed another way of surviving, one that rendered their wings less important. Not only will a little research turn up useful info to make our creations better, but it can give us other ideas and enrich our life as we understand the world around us more.

THE UNIFORMITY ISSUE

Will our fantasy species be able to masquerade as another? A giant spider can't put on a cloak and sneak into a city as if it's a human, unless it can shape shift. A seven-foot species can't pretend they're a three-foot humanoid. The reverse is also true, though two small ones can stand on each other's shoulders and wear a cloak, but you get the idea. Any two species that are similar in appearance, like elves and humans, can try to disguise themselves as the other species, but the more dissimilar they are, the more we deprive ourselves of this option. Decide if you'd like this ability in your work.

Is our species so hostile to others that they aren't allowed in settlements? This reduces them to something few will encounter unless traveling, as our adventurers are likely to do. Would it be more useful if they can be accepted in society, too? If that conflicts with your intention (you like them nasty), we can still achieve this by creating a more benevolent race of them. We'll want a justification for the race, such as the gods created them to counter the existence of the evil species.

The opposite problem can arise: a species so "good" that no one fears or distrusts them. Where's the fun in that? If we create a corrupted race of them that looks the same, people won't always be sure which one they're dealing with. How would this corrupted version originate? A spell, an accident of technology or the supernatural, or they're cursed by someone or something? Does anyone want to "fix" them and how do *they* feel about that idea?

CLOTHING

Typical clothing helps round out appearance and the impression our species creates. Assuming they can acquire clothes made for them, how do they usually dress? Sloppy or refined? Oversized or tailored? Bright colors or drab?

Playfully or seriously? Is there a clothing item associated with them, such as a hat type, scarf, sash, or stylized tunic? How decorated is their attire? Are they inclined to wear symbols of their settlement? Do they have pride in such things?

Even if they go naked, that tells us something about habitat and a likely uninhibited world view. They might have free sexuality; while some associate nudity with sex, this isn't really the case and our species might fit or defy that characterization. Nudity might scandalize more prudish species and form part of their view of each other, the prudes thinking these guys are sexed up (even if not) and these guys thinking the prudes need to lighten up. Such things can provide opportunities to comment on human ideas about sexuality and nudity, enriching our world.

Do they make clothing or are they incapable of such industry? The latter suggests stealing clothes from others and might even be one reason they attack. Any clothes probably fit poorly, are worn, mismatched, and create an impression of chaos and vulgarity. But maybe they buy what they need, assuming there are vendors willing to create and sell to them, possibly exposing themselves to dangers if the species is nefarious; a merchant might get a sword in the chest instead of a handful of gold. Do those vendors get hassled by those who don't want products sold to such a species? This is one way in which world building can lead to characters and story ideas.

ACCESSORIES

Our species might be known for various accessories they're often seen possessing. Maybe they smoke pipes. A flying species might be employed as messengers and have a scroll case or a pouch filled with pen, ink, parchment, and sealing wax. An underground species might be interested in appraising and cutting gems and carry a toolset on their waist. Maybe another travels by foot and goes light, carrying a bindle (sack on a stick). If the species is known for a weapon, this can be part of their typical outfit, such as the sheath or quiver. If they're known to enjoy strong drink, maybe they usually have a flagon with them.

GODS

We arguably need to invent gods before deciding which ones influence our species, but we can start with a general sense of a species disposition and then decide later which deities are likely on their minds. We can be predictable in this, such as deciding that a warlike species worships the god of war, and we likely need to do that, but we can also decide they worship less obvious gods. Maybe they love fate and worship that god, too, despite that god also being the god of truth and integrity, good qualities. This can suggest our species values honor in combat and doesn't do things like stab an opponent in the back. Interpretation is where the fun lies. To think more "outside the box," invent gods first and then your species, then assign them gods and find these conflicts you can resolve in ways that enrich a species.

An important consideration is whether the attributes of our gods influenced the resulting species and their outlook. This not only justifies many aspects but ties different creations together. It also allows us to leverage our existing work, such as the deities. If our gods are organized and those deity groups created a species, then perhaps that species is dominated by the character of those gods. The gods of deception, greed, jealousy, and fear might produce a very different species than the gods of truth, vitality, courage, and intuition. Those examples (daekais and karelia, respectively) are from my work on Llurien, a world with seven groups of gods and seven resulting species. A look at my approach with them on Llurien.com can provide ideas for your world.

CHARACTERISTICS

Anyone familiar with gaming systems has seen a list of characteristics like intelligence, wisdom, charisma, strength, constitution, agility, dexterity, and morale. Each will have a number from one to ten, for example, and a species is rated in each category. The numbering isn't needed for authors, but assigning one can tell us at a glance what we're thinking. We only need a few sentences about each trait and these can be things we never tell our audience. The exercise gets us thinking, and as we write it down, more ideas can occur to us. This example, invented on the fly, demonstrates the kind of work that will be useful to do:

"They aren't the smartest species, having no formal schooling and only learning by word of mouth; their grasp of history is poor. Their street smarts are better, as they can read situations, learning from experience. They lack wisdom, being unable to realize consequences until learning them the hard way. They also don't understand psychology except for how to be menacing, and can be easily lured into traps. They lack charisma, their twisted minds being as repulsive as their bodies, though a certain gleam of excitement does come over them in battle, though only evil people find this attractive.

"Their strength is considerable, allowing them to wield two-handed swords with one hand without fatigue or loss of dexterity. Their constitutions are generally strong in that they have endurance, but they don't heal well and catch sickness easily. Their agility is better than people expect, for they can jump farther and faster than anticipated, but they cannot do acrobatics due to their large size. Dexterity is excellent and they can not only fire all manner of bows with skill but are even gifted musicians, though their music is hideous to other species. Their morale is superior because they have little to no respect for life, whether theirs or someone else's, and feel assured of their place in the afterlife, which is not to say they court death, but dying in battle is an honorable way to go."

WORLD VIEW

One challenge of creating humanoid species is that there's only one here on Earth and we tend to conceptualize invented ones that aren't much different from us. This is natural but maybe not ideal. Many aspects of humanity are taken for granted but can be questioned, turned on their head, and varied to create a world view different from all of humanity, not just one human civilization. We can look to different cultures for inspiration and will do so in *Cultures and Beyond, (The Art of World Building, #3)*. If we want to comment on human assumptions, this affords a great opportunity, especially when human characters on our world encounter our species; it's been noted that fantasy in particular tends to be based on a European model of civilization. The humans are seemingly transplanted from Britain.

To create a different world view, we should avoid having characters react in ways that are identical to humans. While that's a storytelling issue, its roots lie in species conception, or a lack thereof. If we accept that humans are prone to jealousy, and that's how we envision a human character reacting, this can be fine, but if we give an identical reaction to a species that's supposed to be different, this seems like a poor concept. We should question stereotypical reactions of humanity and possibly not give them to our characters at all, not to mention characters of different species.

A good example of this is Spock from *Star Trek*. He reacts differently than the human crew members to almost everything. It often drives ship mates crazy. He gets misunderstood, some calling him arrogant, cold, or worse. It hurts his badly suppressed feelings. It's as much a species clash as a cultural one. The judgmental aspect of humanity goes on display as they vilify a guy they're trying to make sense of, making the human failing of trying to understand another species in human terms.

Decide what your species is like in broad terms. How do they view themselves vs. other species? What is their imagined place in the world? Do others disagree with it? Are they peaceful or a threat to be reckoned with? Do they keep to themselves or travel extensively, and why? What is their reputation? Do they jump to conclusions? Do they react emotionally? Do they trust emotion more than logic, which is viewed with suspicion? Do they take offense at stupid things or overlook them? For all of these things, are they worse or better about it than us? Try not to just make them the same because you haven't thought about it. Make a list of all the stupid aspects of humanity that you've experienced or witnessed (even if it's just in a story), and then figure out how your species would react instead.

Here's an example of the sort of things you might want to write: Diaden see other species as weak both physically and in ability to pursue and realize goals. This has made them disdainful and snobby. Worse, it makes them routinely conquer other species in a belief that it's their job to lead others to a better life. "An unarmed Diaden is a dead one," they're proud of saying, as they're always prepared for battle and put up a terrible fuss if a city has an ordinance against openly carrying weapons, in which case they'll surrender theirs only because more are hidden on them. They disrespect ideas that go against their own. They practice "a good offense is the best defense." Most other species find them pushy, warlike, and confrontational. They seldom have friends among other species, and humans in particular are thought to be evil, for lack of a better word, if keeping company with Diaden.

SOCIETY

What kinds of government does the species typically have? Monarchies, dictatorships, or republics? These are discussed more in *Creating Places (The Art of World Building, #2)*, but those are three of the big ones that can imply levels of sophistication and concern with what we'd call human rights. A society where people can vote government officials in and out of office is markedly different from one where people are executed for dissention. Get a feel for this now and flesh it out later; each of those sovereign power types has varieties we'll examine in Volume 2.

Do your species marry? Do they ever divorce? Their religion might forbid or allow this. There was a time on Earth when the former was expected quite young and the latter almost never happened; we can assign one pair of viewpoints to one species and the reverse to another (having a reason is always a plus, and in a world where armed conflict is common, war can be that justification for either). Are big families the norm or does no one care much about their family? Perhaps they're more like animals in that young are born, raised a few years, and then go on their way, never reuniting. Maybe a child is reared by the whole community and they honor their parents but don't live with them for long. Or maybe they never move out and a home and business is passed down generation after generation.

In modern times, some parts of the world allow some gay marriage, but what about our species' typical society? Is it okay, a crime, or somewhere in between? Do they have abortion? Is abortion government sanctioned and paid for by health care? Are weapons allowed or forbidden? How sophisticated are laws and criminals? This list could go on for forever and we needn't invent everything or we'll never have a life, so choose what you might want to comment on. You can always add to it later.

Our species' habitat will affect their society. A forest-preferring species will likely love plants and woodland animals. A sea-dwelling species is the same for sea life. They might have less contact with other species, being more innocent, ignorant of their evils, and trusting; this might be true of an underground species. A flying species likely has more contact with everyone and is very social, maybe acting as messengers or scouts in human society. These will affect society and the overall outlook of a species.

LANGUAGES

Does your species have a written language? Did they invent it, or is it based on another species' language? This will affect how likely it is for two species to share a tongue that has diverged in some way. Is a written language words, symbols, or a combination? Less sophisticated species tend to have symbols. Those without a written language will be less educated, sophisticated, and have less sense of history, being unable to write it down.

We might have little reason to mention this, but is the language written right to left, top to bottom, or something else? There's one plausible theory for why differences exist: earliest writing was chipped into stone, and with most Earth people being right-handed, the chisel was held in the left hand so that it made sense to start on the right. When writing on parchment (or something similar) was introduced, going right to left increased the chance of smudging the writing, so left to right took over. But it's just a theory.

Can they speak, read, and write other languages? Which ones and to what degree of fluency? A flying species might be well traveled and pick up a smattering of many languages. A species that seldom goes anywhere, like elves and mountain dwarves, might not care about becoming bilingual, or they might learn a common tongue in distaste. They could pride themselves on their ignorance. Regionally, one population of a species might be different from another in many ways, including languages.

In SF, the use of universal translators has rendered this subject less important. It's a practical matter for film and TV shows to reduce or eliminate the need for subtitles and invented languages. Authors don't have this issue as much. The "universal" aspect of this doesn't need to be taken literally, as there can and likely should be languages that such a device hasn't been programmed with yet. This is truer for stories where characters are entering seemingly unexplored areas of the cosmos, as anywhere within explored areas is likely included already.

These devices are not typically shown as being able to scan text and translate it, but they would likely have the technology. Our characters may have picked up the ability to read a few key words or symbols in other tongues, but with universal translators abounding, they would have little reason to learn to speak or understand one. Regardless of what we decide, we can always have such a device fail, be lost, or be destroyed so that our characters are reduced to the old-fashioned way of trying to understand an unknown language: with great difficulty.

Is there a common tongue most species can speak if not read and write? If so, where did that language originate? In *Creating Places (The Art of World Building, #2)*, we'll look into creating sovereign powers; that will be a good time to invent an empire, which is a disparate group of sovereign powers united under one power that forces cultural changes on other, previously independent ones. The name of the empire might also be the name of the language that becomes the common tongue, at least in that region or continent. For example, "Antarian" is the common tongue of my Llurien world, named as much for the defunct Empire of Antaria as for the continent Antaria where all life originated; the language is that of the humans.

Cultures and Beyond (The Art of World Building, #3), looks into whether you should create a language and how.

CUSTOMS

Inventing customs, or leveraging Earth analogues, can help bring a species to life. Greetings, farewells, dining, and spiritual habits are all good subjects that will figure in our storytelling. Differences between this species and others can cause a misunderstanding, which has often been done in the *Star Trek* universe to the point of being a cliché, but it still affords us a chance to question human assumptions, which can in turn enlighten our audience. This is an opportunity to explore options other than those we've grown up with.

Actual customs can include shaking hands, holding doors for people, and ceremonies about birth, death, burial, weddings, and divorce. In a warlike story, soldiers might have customs regarding leaving their family, starting service, going into battle, mourning a comrade, and bringing a body home. Religion almost always has a number of customs associated with it.

This subject will be revisited in more depth in *Cultures and Beyond, (The Art of World Building, #3)*.

HISTORY

A history improves world building, but the one for our species doesn't need to be elaborate. An early decision should be where they first appeared. We might have decided this was a forest, but which one? On what continent? If we only have one land mass, the one we're intending to build out and use, that's easier, but we can still name another continent and never (or later) do things like create a map. If they originated from somewhere other than where we intend to tell our story, do we have an idea why they're here? Did all of them migrate, or did only some, resulting in at least two groups that might have biologically diverged over millennia the way humans did on Earth? This gives us races of the species.

It might give us corresponding attitudes, too. After deciding where the original territory was, we can get an idea of how new each additional group is based on geography. For example, Europeans spread around the world only to discover other races, which were then conquered by military might or even disease to which the native races didn't have immunity. If your species did this, it can create conflict with those they live among now, just as Native Americans are in conflict with the society Britain originally brought here. This is a simple justification for your species having issues with others.

Those who haven't left their original location much will have a world view reflecting this. It can manifest as skepticism that places they've heard of are real. It can make them suspicious of outsiders. They could feel abandoned by anyone who left. They might feel the departed are wayward and should be brought back into the fold. War may force them out and into a world they're poorly equipped to navigate, literally and figuratively.

Wars are another subject to devote time to as these events are remembered for centuries, causing long lasting attitudes, even when two former foes put aside their differences and become reluctant allies, possibly against another threat. Conquest also causes the conquering species to leave an impact on those they dominate, even long after that dominance ends; a language can become common to both, as can customs. Don't go overboard, however, because we'll likely have little opportunity to use much of it.

Has this species been conquered and/or enslaved in the past? Was it their own species or another? Are they still this way or did they gain their freedom, when, and how? Did others come to their aid or did they do it themselves? What we're really after are events to give them attitudes about others.

If you just started creating your first species, you might have to return to this later, when you can think about how you want them to get along. Just make up issues that have boiled over into outright confrontation. Fighting over resources like forests and other land features is a great start because it has more to do with needs than attitude. Depriving others of access to trade routes, or allowing it, can cause animosity or friendliness. Attacks and rescues do the same. Two species can mostly get along, like humans and elves, but still dislike each other over imagined slights, attitudes, and misunderstandings. Look to human history for inspiration. We can google any conflict to learn why it happened, then leverage that idea.

RELATIONSHIPS

Unless this species is the only one in our work, we need to decide how they relate to humans and other species of our invention, or any public domain species we're using. Inventing this tends to be easier when we've created other aspects first, like appearance, habitat, and world view. Ideas can form during those processes. Giving this time and not forcing it can help, as can imagining interactions as if we're writing scenes between them and others. Then think about why you have them acting the way they do. Use various situations that are likely to occur, such as greetings, farewells, dining etiquette, and how they react to various kinds of news that impacts their fortunes.

We must be sure to decide how two invented species interact. Using elves and dwarves as examples, it's easy to fall prey to deciding how humans get along with elves and dwarves but not deciding how elves and dwarves get along with each other. A single paragraph is often enough to get started. We're looking for high level ideas. Anything more detailed can arise while creating stories.

Are they enemies? Friends? Why? Are their legendary battles or animosities? Treaties? Are they allies now but some among them have bad blood? Every species should have opinions and prejudice about others, and humans should feel or think something stereotypical about everything we create (because we do that). There should be classic misunderstandings. Some of our characters should exemplify these ideas while others rise above them. It adds conflict and dimension. We can start with Earth analogues.

Is it normal for one to smash furniture on hearing bad news? Punch a wall? Or react stoically as if nothing has occurred? While these have nothing to do with relation-ships, the way others perceive them is certainly affected and in turn impacts relationships. If our species literally kills messengers, others aren't going to send them, for example, unless wanting to get rid of someone that way. More to the point, the species would be see as temperamental by others and this will change how people deal with them. Reputations are born of such things.

A well done species can allow the author to make commentary about humans, which in turn helps our audience relate to our work. We can craft our species to do this. Feel we're dishonest? Make your species honest. Think we jump to conclusions? Make your species slow and deliberate in its evaluations to the point that it bugs humans. If you think humans are faithful to gods, create a species that is quick to turn its back on gods if not answered, making us look good by comparison. Maybe our species doesn't understand the concept of property and just takes other people's stuff like it's no big deal and we accuse them of being thieves. Any social or cultural expectation of ours be turned on its head, an opposite expectation given to another species to cause conflict with not only humans, but other species.

SUPERNATURAL

If our world has the supernatural, we should decide our species' relationship with it. First we'll need to decide how prevalent these forces are; this is covered in more detail in *Cultures and Beyond (The Art of World Building, #3)*. In a world where magic is rare, everyone is probably a little wary of it while also wishing they had such power. In a world where it's common, it might be as unnoticed as electricity is to us. One approach is to decide how much supernatural there is in general, then how much our species is involved with it, and finally how much experience our character has. The reverse method also works, though this is arguably more suited to a world that's invented for a specific tale. The intelligence and morale of our species will greatly impact their relationship with the supernatural, which can be divided into two groups: seemingly natural phenomena and ones caused by people (aka, magic).

PHENOMENA

What does our species think and feel about super-natural places? Are these to be avoided or sought out? The answer might depend on what kind of phenomenon it is. Something that perverts everything or everyone who goes near will naturally repel most people, but maybe we have a species that is unaffected by such things. Or maybe they take it upon themselves to investigate and neutralize them. It adds a great dynamic if everyone else runs away and this species runs toward it.

Imagine how this affects what others think of them. Are they crazy? Suicidal? Evil? Saviors? Honorable? Do they do something unspeakable with whatever they find at the heart of these places? Do they trap something causing it? If so, what do they do with it? Is that thing alive? Are they preventing further horrors? We can have characters who don't fit typical behaviors, but first we'll need to know what that typifies.

Does our species have special protection, weapons, or other devices? This is only likely if they're the ones designing them, unless they've made their willingness to do these things known and others have created things for them. Do those devices fall into the wrong hands and lead to other problems, including foolish people thinking they can now do what this species can, only to wreak havoc?

Our species might be less or more affected by a phenomena than others. We don't need a reason, although in SF, a scientist is probably trying to figure that out. We're talking about imaginary phenomena, which gives us creative license to invent pseudo-science. Sometimes having a mystery is good, however, and if we ever reveal our invented truth, long hidden, it had better be good. Remember the collective groan when the *Star Wars* universe named the thing that gives some people the ability to use the force. A mundane explanation to something that appears mystical and magical is arguably a mistake.

MAGIC

Whether we call them wizards, sorcerers, or something else, decide whether the species is likely to become magicians. This can be influenced by how magic works on our world. There seem to be two varieties of wizards: those who can do magic by force of will like a god, and those who must learn spells, with the requisite words, gestures, and physical materials and preparation needed for each. Our world might have both, giving us some flexibility.

This distinction matters because spells are often depicted as requiring schooling, discipline, and access to needed materials, which are often exotic and therefore hard to acquire. An uneducated species might have the aptitude for magic but lack the training or materials. Or if they're nefarious, perhaps no one will teach them. Education might come not from schools and guilds but individual tutors, who can in turn exact brutal requirements from an apprentice, holding the quest for power over their heads and making them earn their trade after performing terrible acts.

The species might not have access to spell materials without dangerous quests to get them or paying exorbitant fees to buy them. A nearby wizard's tower might be a seemingly good source of what they need, except that any magician with half a brain would fortify their dwelling. Rare items are often regarded as allowing for more powerful magic, so our species might be prevented from great power by difficulty attaining what they need.

Is our species disciplined enough to learn spells?

Compare their impulsiveness to humanity's and make a decision. Those who easily give in to frustration might not succeed at all in casting spells or might do a poor job of it, causing unintended side effects to themselves, others, or their surroundings. Is this chaos the reason they're feared?

If our species can't read, casting spells seems less likely, given the need for learning from a spell book, for example. If they can read their language or "common," can they read magic words? This is usually considered higher learning and someone would have to teach them, unless there's a simple spell that would allow them to read anything. There are ways around these issues, should we decide we want a character who's an exception. We can also decide that spells can be taught orally and memorized.

By contrast, wielding supernatural power without spells or materials, just by imagining something and drawing power from around us, may require none of these things. A disadvantaged species could have powerful but undisciplined, and therefore very dangerous, wizards. They likely don't care about a teacher. Maybe they're arrogant.

But we shouldn't make them too powerful without explanation. Usually magicians are given limitations in fiction to prevent them from being unstoppable. It can also humanize them. A common and believable limitation is that it takes energy to perform spells. Wizards save their strength for more worthy moments. Someone cocky might have no problem with wiping out defenseless people, but someone with pride might also see this as beneath them and let their henchmen do it.

There could be side effects to what they're doing, whether to themselves, others, or the world, with them largely ignorant of or indifferent to this. Do they learn of it the hard way? Do they resist such an inconvenient truth if others try to tell them? Do they know and don't care? Because they're evil or because their survival is more important? Do other species try to assassinate such wizards when one is known to exist?

A benevolent species is arguably more inclined toward

civilization and therefore schooling, discipline, and access to at least more mundane supplies. Do they refuse to teach a nefarious species or do they do so anyway, knowing the problems this could cause and either not caring or doing it on purpose for some reason? Maybe one of our evil species is indeed well educated, etc., and teaches what they can do to less educated but no less evil species.

GODLY POWER

The gods, should they exist in our world, typically have powers they'll grant to a species. A classic scenario is a species laying hands on someone and channeling a god's power to heal the wounded. The power can be used in other ways, but whatever it is, this is different from magic as defined above because it's an issue of faith and not skill.

A species that lacks all that's required to become a wizard can achieve power through faith, leveling the playing field, though they're at the mercy of their god to answer their prayers. Might this not make them quite devoted, to augment their chances? This suggests a deeply religious species, or at least for some of its members. This can influence their relationships with others and their own kind, the priests reigning condemnation down on non-believers and trying to convert people, for example.

Whether evil or good, gods like attention and reward faith with their power. Imagine a god of cynicism who is also a god of poison and sickness, who grants his priest the ability to make someone wither and die from twenty paces. A god of innocence might be able to counter this by offering their priest the power of rejuvenation. Species can become part of a proxy war, caught in the middle but realizing it (or not) and taking what they can get. The role of priests can become quite strong but depends on a well-developed pantheon (see Chapter Two, "Creating Gods").

TECHNOLOGY

FANTASY

In a fantasy setting, technology means things like forging steel weapons, plate armor, or chainmail—the trade of blacksmiths, who are held in high regard. There are more rudimentary elements that our audience is unlikely to care about, including plumbing, irrigation, aqueducts, water wheels, and general tools for farming (a wood plow vs. an iron one). These are generally assumed to exist, but the question here is whether our new species is capable of such industry. Do they have architects smart enough to build structures that withstand storms and earthquakes? Can they build fortifications? Is the technological level enough to create more sanitary living conditions?

If not, they'll have to go without, live among those who do, or get these things by other means, whether stealing, buying, or conquering. They might have allies who'll agree to trade and train them in how to achieve something on their own.

SCIENCE FICTION

In SF, we think of technology as being far in advance of our own on Earth, not the sort of rudiments mentioned under the fantasy section above. Is our species able to design and build machines of any kind, not to mention something far beyond current human capacity? This requires intelligence, education and infrastructure for mining, refinement, chemistry, and more. Do we envision that they're chemists, engineers, and physicists? If not, they must steal everything, with it being more likely that they'll steal an entire ship, for example, rather than the parts to assemble one; this would be true of most if not all other technologies.

Can we assume that some of these intellectual capacities and skills, like engineering, are needed to operate machines? That depends on our goal. Creators often grant spaceships advanced artificial intelligence (A.I.) that takes care of many functions. This gives a less than brilliant species far more opportunities, just as a gun allows a child to kill a samurai. Do the builders of these machines account for that and require more intelligence to operate something, or biometric security? A good approach would be a mix of these styles so that we can decide, based on our story needs, which option is in effect. For example, one species could make everything easy to operate while another does not. A third species that is contemplating stealing something would take this into consideration.

Decide what their life with technology is like. An ignorant and uneducated species can enjoy life in space even if they're not in command, because every space ship needs janitors, for example. This subservient position is something to keep in mind because it greatly broadens opportunities for them. While they might be in unenviable positions, they can still get around, and there's the mutiny idea of such a species taking over despite their limited technological skills. Maybe they bribe ship's officers into helping them. With some ingenuity, we can find a way to empower a weaker species.

Maybe our species steals or captures ships and is smart enough to operate but not maintain them; if something goes wrong, the crew might be stranded. Are they known for having to send out distress calls over this? It would likely get them captured and arrested, but they probably know all about this problem and travel in pairs, for example, the still-functional ship rescuing the other's crew before everyone flees. They might also set traps, taking over a ship that comes to help them, whether they really need that help or were just setting someone up.

More advanced species will be the ones inventing technology and trying to safeguard it. They'll be the victims of ruses by those species who can't create these things. How has this changed or hardened/softened attitudes and laws about theft and tampering? With biometrics, devices could be set to only work with one species. We can invent all sorts of safeguards and ways of defeating them.

Not every species' society which lacks the ability to create technology will be "evil." Some might need the protection of another benevolent species. They might be taken advantage of by a nefarious one. There can be attempts to exterminate them or make them slaves. Fear about such outcomes could drive them to seek alliances, which may carry risks of their own.

If our species lack a society capable of producing technology (of whatever sophistication level), they may still be part of a mixed-species society that does indeed have the sophistication to create technological wonders. In this scenario, the smarter members of our species might be capable of gaining education, unless the society forbids them from doing so; a reason for that restriction is preferred, such as misuse of advanced information in the past. If our species can gain skills needed, they could introduce them to their own society with one degree of success or another.

COMBAT

Deciding on our species' morale, society, personality, and body (including dexterity, agility, strength, and constitution), will help determine combat skills. A species that prides itself on "a good death" is unlikely to run or retreat. This might inspire more ferocity on the battlefield. But if there's no shame in running, and they run faster than everything else, perhaps our species has few battle skills, excelling at hiding and diversionary tactics.

Lack of dexterity and refinement reduce the likelihood of our species using bows except for the crossbow. Lack of finesse needed for the sword might have them pre-ferring crushing weapons. A large species with big hands might be unable to wield many things designed for smaller species, but a club, mace, or staff could fit their hands better. A short species won't be using spears, long bows, or staves designed for anyone larger.

A flying species will likely use slings and other missile weapons so as to avoid bringing their wings into range of hand-to-hand weapons, but a bow might not be the easiest thing to carry unless it's small. Arrows in a quiver will need to be secured to prevent them from falling out, causing a delay each time they want to grab one. Rocks are often suggested as projectiles for slings, but rocks can become heavy unless their numbers are reduced, which in turn limits the number of attacks and might inspire our species to become quite accurate.

Does our species hunt others or get hunted? Does this occur for food, sport, or trophies? Decide how skilled they are at detecting threats or avoiding them. Do they stalk prey? Decide if they work in groups with their own kind or prefer going it alone. How do group tactics differ? Maybe they have special attacks or defenses. A species with a barbed tail might use it only for defense against a rear attack or might whip it forward. Maybe it's poisoned, and if so, do they sting someone and sit back and wait for them to die or become immobile? Can they spit fire or something corrosive?

WHERE TO START

A top-down approach to inventing a species means viewing a species at a high level and working our way into details. We might decide on a sea-dwelling species and then face more detailed questions, like whether they have gills or can survive out of water. Can they walk on land? Are they seen often or rarely?

The bottom-up approach means creating details first and then slowly integrating them into a unified whole. Maybe we first decide on a species with sharp claws, a barbed tail, and which is rumored to carry people off at night while seldom being seen, and there's almost no trace of where it went. From this and other details, perhaps we decide this species is water-dwelling and the claws and tail are used for catching fish. The reason people disappear is that they're taken underwater and drowned, or perhaps held captive in underwater caves that have oxygen pockets, and since our species quickly enters the water from docks, there's no trail to follow. This big picture is suggested by details we created first.

4

---•••---

CREATING WORLD FIGURES

No book on world building would be complete without mention of those who live there, as they are arguably the whole point. That said, the creation of people will depend on our goals. If we're world building for gaming, then our world needs characters for the gamers to interact with. If we're a writer, then characters might be best suited to the stories we intend to tell.

Since this isn't a book on writing, I won't delve into the details of building memorable characters, because the goal of this chapter is to create well-known figures. Nonetheless, much of what follows can help us build characters. These are people we can reference at any time but which might not figure into a story. For example, on Earth we have Elvis, Oprah Winfrey, Tom Cruise, Tom Brady, Jesus Christ, Hitler, and the boy who cried wolf. In other words, a musician, television personality, actor, athlete, religious figure, dictator, and cautionary tale. In our world, we might replace them with wizard, knight, priest, and martyr. Or star fighter, bounty hunter, emperor, and Jedi knight.

Appendix 3 is a template for creating a world figure. It includes more comments and advice, and an editable file can be downloaded for free by joining the newsletter at http://www.artofworldbuilding.com/newsletter/

TYPES

Our world could benefit from heroes, villains, martyrs, and others who've become famous for whatever reason, such as physical traits, supernatural ones, or their role in world events. There isn't much difference between one type and another when it comes to inventing them, aside for the reason they're famous. Figure out what sorts of individuals are likely to be well remembered. This will give us a list of people to invent. Adding a touch of detail to the list will help inspire us. For example:

- A knight who turned the tide of war, maybe by sacrificing himself
- A knight who restored tarnished honor in the knighthood by doing something heroic
- A wizard who made people fear wizards
- An assassin who killed an emperor and triggered war (or stopped it)
- A passionate priest and good orator who inspired many to follow a god or way of life
- An influential leader who was assassinated or martyred, causing great social change
- A dictator who wanted to exterminate a race and caused large scale war
- A warrior known for incredible prowess but brought down by mundane health concerns
- A famous explorer whose ship vanished

If you're wondering where I got those, here are inspirations in no particular order: Martin Luther King,

Bruce Lee, *The Princess Bride, Dragonlance*, and Hitler. By summing them up without their names, we start making them our own and continue by creating details.

FAME

Our character is famous for something. This is the reason we're creating them. What are we hoping to achieve? Do we want someone whose name people fear to invoke? Someone to inspire others in times of trouble? Someone who is an example, good or bad, of what's possible? These motives (for us) needn't be dependent on stories we intend to tell. Our purpose is to have someone for our characters to admire, so what we need at the outset is a basic purpose for this person and how and why they are so revered or loathed. This can be a one liner in our notes: "He said a prayer to Lord Vallen, who at the Battle of Westin saved King Harin at the cost of his life and in so doing restored honor to the tarnished knighthood."

Whatever our character's fame, there are bound to be details about them, their life, their story, and even what they did that people are wrong about. Maybe others have wishful thinking that someone was a certain way. People idolize heroes, ignoring ugly details, such as adultery or alcoholism. People demonize villains and ignore that they might've been truly devoted to their children. These exaggerations are part of humanity, at the least. When inventing your person, decide what people have right and wrong about them. Are there little known facts that might (or might not) change how they're viewed?

DEAD OR ALIVE

Decide if they're dead or still alive. If deceased, are they really dead or just presumed so? How did they die and was this satisfying in some way to the audience or characters? They could be incorrectly identified as dead and just be missing. If so, decide who the last person to see them was. Maybe they faked their death. We should have a reason and decide on the circumstances of that. What will cause them to return?

Are they imprisoned and is that known or not? If jailed or exiled, decide where, for how long, and why. The prison may have special properties or a unique location. How do they feel about being jailed (i.e., is it justified and do they agree?)? Maybe there's a release date everyone's worried about and preparing for. Have people become complacent about the threat this person poses so that they're easy prey when he returns without warning?

If the character is still alive, are they retired in old age, or out and about still doing things to add to that fame? Are they okay with that fame or hiding from it? Does anyone think they're past their prime? And how does our person feel about being viewed that way? Do they resent it or agree, perhaps sheepishly?

Our world has history and some if not most of these figures will be long gone (or at least thought to be—immortality, or the near equivalent, gives us options). Characters we'll never use except as a reference don't need much development, so when filling out the template in the appendix, don't spend too much time on each section. It's living people that benefit from more thought.

We might decide someone is too much fun and we'll keep them around, changing their status to living, but this can cause a problem if we've tied the events of their life to the events of our world history and can't change it. But we can always write a story set in the past.

POSSESSIONS

A hero or villain with cool stuff excites the imagination. Who doesn't like Jedi Knights with light sabers (*Star Wars*)? Or albino weaklings with a sword that devours souls and transfers the victim's energy to the wielder (*Elric of Melnibone*)? Or a warrior with a fierce bird that would devour lesser men but obeys him (Tarl Carbot of the *Gor Series*)? Run of the mill items are nothing to get excited over and won't become famous and are probably not what we're looking for here. Jewelry, weapons, and animals can all be memorable possessions, but it's arguably better to choose one or two for each character. Otherwise the law of diminishing returns kicks in and the impact of each item becomes diluted by the existence of the others.

When deciding what our character has/had, consider giving them something suited to our purpose and their status. If they're a warrior, a weapon is an obvious choice. This can be one that achieved a famous result (such as it's the sword/gun that killed a certain bad guy) or one that was just generally used by them and had a special property that made it famous. Maybe the weapon was altered in some way, either a piece removed or something added to alter its functionality, power, or speed.

Armor is less exciting. Armor that saved our guy makes them a little weak, by comparison; we like people who save themselves. But it might allow them to enter something like a supernatural phenomenon no one else could enter, for example. But if the armor became cursed—or was all along—that's better, especially if it's still around on our world or believed destroyed (but isn't). What if the armor compelled them to do dangerous missions, as if it had a mind of its own? This is one way to meld a famous character with a famous item.

An item they are always seen with can also acquire a mythic reputation. A wizard's staff comes to mind, as does any outfit they typically wear or an item they use on their adventures. Something small like a ring is unlikely to capture much attention unless it has a giant diamond in it, for example. A necklace or belt are progressively more likely to get noticed, as is anything worn on the head.

Broken items are another area of interest. Can it be put back together? Some or all of the pieces might be lost. Decide who broke it, why and when, what led to this, and the aftermath. Was there a defeated hero/villain, a chaotic artifact, or explosion (one that created a monster)?

How did our character acquire this item? Maybe it was found on an adventure, bestowed, or forged for them. It could be standard equipment that just has a fearsome reputation. Have they ever lost it and if so, with what consequences? Did they recover it? Perhaps it's no longer the same or has changed in some way, which might be significant. It could still be useable or dangerous in the wrong kind of way now. They may keep the altered item out of loyalty. Did anything happen to our character because they no longer had it?

If the item is still lost, is our character looking for it or have they given it up? Do you intend them to find it? Do you have any ideas who has it now? Are there any consequences if someone ill-equipped to handle it has it? This can apply to items that our gods have as well. In addition to weapons, armor, clothing, books, and devices to help with mundane or extraordinary tasks like food, shelter, and communication, we also have steeds and ships to consider (see the next section).

Did they get it by gambling? Maybe it was a trade deal, such as someone selling it without having any idea of its true value, which was then discovered by our character. The possession could have been the result of a quest our character went on specifically to find it.

Do others covet the item, causing our character to need to protect it? Either way, in a world with thousands of years of history, there are plenty of interesting items to be found and which no longer belong to their original owner; this goes up exponentially across multiple planets.

We might want to figure out who created the item. Did our character do it themselves? This is more likely if they're a wizard or engineer. We can also create a history for this item making its way through multiple hands, possibly causing problems along the way, most famously with our character?

STEEDS AND SHIPS

Steeds and ships (especially in SF) have a special place as a companion or a trusted way out of tricky situations. Audiences can become attached to them (like the Millennium Falcon of *Star Wars*), and that's what we want. Find a way to give it personality, which generally starts with a good name. If this is an animal, the way to make an audience care about it is to make the animal seem to care about our character, such as coming to the rescue, being loyal, and following orders, even showing initiative. Just like with dogs, we admire an animal loyal to a person, plus one who can be counted on. Sometimes having the animal injured, and the character to be upset about that, allows us to care, too. There is probably at least one famous dragon, horse, or enormous bird on your world, if they exist at all.

Ships have personality even if they're the non-AI man-o-war type of our Earth past. This has to do with characterization and other characters assigning traits to an inanimate object, so this might be harder in a video game. The more people consider it their home, the more personal a ship becomes. A great name is a huge benefit here and must not be overlooked.

With artificial intelligence, ships can be a step up from fantasy without talking AI. Sense of humor and banter go a long way with making an audience like the AI. If that AI is not perfect, making mistakes or being too invasive with unwanted body scans, for example, this humanizes them and can add humor. We can treat an AI as if it's a human (or other species) but with limitations on understanding emotions or physical impacts of a body on one's state of mind, disposition, and attitude; in other words, maybe they don't understand our character as well as they think. An AI can also become corrupted or be taken over by outsiders, and while obvious, it's still a good idea provided our version is done well. Talking ships are not the same as talking swords, too; we can get away with this one whereas an audience will skewer us for a talking sword.

The creation of AI is covered in *Cultures and Beyond (The Art of World Building, #3)*.

RELATIONSHIPS

When creating a world figure, their relationships may not be that important to us if we'll do little more than have a character name-drop their hero. This can be an area to skimp on until later, if ever, but should we decide to invent their relationships, this section may help. Some people are famous for who they kept company with, including who their enemies were.

FAMILY

Parents, siblings, lovers, and children (and extended family) all provide benefit or add risk to heroes and villains alike, so decide who is in our character's life. Or what happened to those people if gone. Did family die first, breaking our character's spirit, or did family outlive him and mourn our dead character, possibly wanting revenge on a killer or responsible party? One of those mourners might be even more interesting than the person we started creating. A family of evildoers can be a lot of fun. A family of heroes can make us root for the lot of them. A family with both is even better.

If they have children, do they know about all of them? It's a cliché to have an unknown child turn up, so you might want to avoid that. Television shows, especially soap operas, desperate for a surprise twist, have ruined that. The unknown sibling is equally cheesy, so if we're going that route, make it good, interesting, and plausible. After all, it actually *does* happen, but we might want to only do that once in an entire writing career. If we need to introduce someone later, it's better to admit our character knew that the person existed and it just didn't come up in a story due to irrelevance (before now). Try to avoid playing the unknown relative card.

Has our villain been disavowed by relatives? This might be some or all of them. Some relatives might offer safe harbor at the risk of being cast out by the rest, or punished by society. What's in it for them to risk this? Perhaps they truly love our villain and feel they can save him one day. A mother who can't give up on her baby, now an adult, is overdone but understandable. Less common is a mother who has turned on their child. Potent emotions can be the reason our villain went bad in the first place.

Then there's our hero, who might wish to make family proud but whose actions have put family members in harm's way. Heroes have powerful enemies and there's no telling what some will do to family. Has our hero hidden children or a lover to protect them? Do the protected ones chafe at this? What kind of stress has arisen between hero and family due to this? Has anyone died despite our hero's attempt to protect them, and what effect did this have on them? Are they guilt ridden? Did they quit and let the evil they swore to stop go unchallenged, letting it win, and if so, what did it do to our hero? Destroy him? Is he a drunk now, unable to take all the guilt? Will he be redeemed one day? Are the children old enough to have a life of their own and cause trouble for their hero parent in other ways, as only teenagers can?

This raises a final point that is often overlooked—there are descendants of this person. Maybe one of our story's characters is that descendant, whether one generation later or dozens. If other characters know that, it can be something they want to downplay. These relatives may have changed their name or done something to hide their association, and this may have worked for most people but not fooled everyone, possibly with consequences down the road. A common idea is of a deceased relative coming back from the grave to inhabit the body of a relative, so be clever if going that familiar route.

THE SPECIES

Since our character is famous, he's likely famous outside of his own species. With each species having a different world view, each might view this person differently. A hero to some will be a villain to others. Be sure to think about this to give your character added dimension. While elves and dwarves might view the character positively, each might have gripes about it. By contrast, ogres and goblins might view the individual as evil but again have slightly different issues with them.

While creating deeds for our character, keep in mind that they may have run into conflict with one or more species while undertaking a mission. This can range from obvious encounters with ogres, for example, to enthusiastic help from elves and grudging aid from dwarves. Or the latter could've been openly hostile to what they wanted to do, not allowing our character to enter their lands, forcing him to take the long way around, for example. Make sure everything wasn't easy for them or there wouldn't be a reason they're famous.

HISTORY

ORIGINS, DEMISE, AND IN BETWEEN

While we don't need every last detail of where a character came from, it helps to know their original continent, at the least, and preferably a kingdom, too. The latter might wait until we've invented more and decided on the governments and quality of life there, as discussed in detail in *Creating Places (The Art of World Building, #2)*. Decide whether they still live there, have taken up residence elsewhere, or became a wanderer. Create a quick reason for their choice, which may have been influenced by familial concerns, such as keeping relatives safe by going far away and lying about origins. Or if the government made life horrible for people, they might have left. Or maybe life was wonderful and they left to help those less fortunate.

Our choices will impact much about their worldview, assuming we've created cultures as detailed in *Cultures and Beyond (The Art of World Building, #3)*. The society they came from will have beliefs and customs, and while the latter is not hugely important, the former is. There are basic ideas about how life should be lived, such as how different genders are treated. This is more important for characters that we intend to use as more than a reference, but if the Kingdom of Norn viewed woman as little more than sex objects and our male hero is from there, this would impact how well he gets along with people in other cultures that differ. Is this the reason he couldn't get along with peers and worked alone, for example?

Once we've decided where they came from, decide where they've lived or even if they just kept moving as if in search of something. Having multiple sovereign powers they've been influenced by helps create personality. This is another thing we needn't worry about too much at first (if at all) unless planning to use their residence in some way, such as a story where people end up there. Their home might have booby traps, whether mundane, technological, or magical. In SF, surveillance from a distance is likely, but we can still do this in fantasy with spells or magic devices. Decide how simple or majestic their home is. Personality will figure into this, but so will the fame heaped upon them and whether they've monetarily benefited from their exploits or not.

If the character is dead, decide where the remains and any special items they possessed are. Is the body intact? Is it ashes? Is that grave actually empty but few if any know it? Maybe their grave is guarded, revered, or haunted. Their items can be buried with them or hidden. Maybe the items are lost, or just believed lost, and someone secretly has them, though it can be more interesting if more than one person has the various items, especially if they are needed together.

If they're still alive, where are they living now? What are they doing with their time? Are they hunted and living with lots of protection, or are they celebrated and afraid old enemies will destroy those they love? Are they imprisoned? Living world figures can be fun, though maybe nothing beats undead ones.

TRAINING AND SKILLS

While some individuals have innate skills, notable people like wizards, knights, gunfighters, and pilots often have training. We don't need a lot of details here, but decide if they went to an academy of some kind. Consider where it was, and whether they graduated, fit in or not, and if they're considered a great example of the academy's graduates or an embarrassment to the institution. Some of this will play into personality. They might've been apprenticed to a master, and if so, did they part ways peacefully? Does the master approve of him? Or did our character kill his master for his secrets or some slight, real or imagined? And is anyone after our person for justice or revenge? This could be the reason they're famous.

Another way to gain skills is by being captured and trained for something like gladiator fights. Or being conscripted into an army or as a sailor. Some of their skills can have less to do with fighting and magic, and more to do with navigation and tracking, wilderness survival, and the customs of various kingdoms. The latter brings up another point that some skills are gained in the field, whether military or social, instead of in a training regime. Unless our character was royalty, nobility, or aristocracy, they likely weren't trained in the finer points of etiquette, but they could still be a quick study, emulating what they see, though not without some gaffes.

Street smarts are either earned, innate, or both. Whether

our character has this or not would help determine their effectiveness, whether it's actually being good on the streets or just the ability to read people and situations. Being bad at this might also cause them trouble that sours them on relationships and turns them into a villain.

DEEDS

The reason our character is known is presumably what they've done, though they can be famous for what they are, such as the last of a royal line or an exiled princess. Characters who never do anything aren't terribly interesting, however, so give some thought to actions this individual has taken. Actions that changed the world are ideal. For example, if we want magic badly restricted but don't have a reason, perhaps a villain wizard killed an emperor with this restriction as a consequence all must pay. Perhaps they've destroyed a kingdom, ruined a virgin princess by seducing her, or killed a terrifying warlord. Think about what you want them to have accomplished and make a list that can be as simple and short as below, and which can be expanded on further should the need ever arise:

1. Destroyed a given magic or technological item of great importance so that two or more groups would stop fighting to get it, earning a burn on one side of the face when it exploded
2. Invaded a given kingdom and turned the tide of power so that the kingdom fell
3. Recovered a lost weapon which they became known for wielding
4. As ship captain, destroyed a fleet and turned the tide of war

WHERE TO START

The first fundamental decision is what type of person are we inventing: good or evil? While it's true that some will consider a person one way while others consider them another, it's easier for us to decide on one to start with and decide later how enemies might view them. We should also decide their profession, such as knight, warrior, priest, or ruler. This will determine their capabilities and often how traveled they are, plus their influence. Next we should decide what we're hoping to achieve with this person. Remember that they aren't necessarily a character we'll use in a prominent way (we can do that later of course), but someone whose existence influenced the world and inhabitants. The deeds for which they became famous are often central to this, so focus on what they've done. Another major decision is how long ago they lived and died, or whether they're still alive. Other items can be saved for last, including possessions, steeds, ships, family, relationships, origins, and training.

5

———•••·———

CREATING MONSTERS

A world with monsters is arguably more entertaining than one without.

Appendix 4 is a template for creating one. It includes more comments and advice, and an editable file can be downloaded for free by signing up for the newsletter at http://www.artofworldbuilding.com/newsletter/

DEFINING MONSTER

We all know what a monster is, but since we might be creating species and animals, too, let's be clear. The term implies something harmful, unnatural, and morally objectionable, whether there's a physical deformity or psychological one. Monsters aren't real, of course, and are created by storytellers, usually to depict or highlight some of the above, sometimes as a warning. They are often a freak of nature and can result from birth defects, in which case it was something else, like a human, before being regarded as a monster by horrified onlookers. Their existence has often been thought to foreshadow something evil happening, which is one reason they are cast out.

In science fiction and fantasy, the word "sentient" is used to describe creatures that are human-like in their mental capabilities, even though that's not what the word really means. Due to this convention, this usage will be retained herein anyway. The real definition of sentient only includes the ability to sense, feel, and experience, which means an animal is technically sentient.

As a side note, with space traveling characters visiting new planets, what they might term a monster at first might turn out to be an indigenous animal. Either that, or it's a member of a species that might've been stranded, for example, and terrifies those near through no fault of its own except appearance, and it's assumed to be a monster.

MONSTERS VS. SPECIES

The difference between a monster and an intelligent species is arguably their minds. A humanoid species is typically sophisticated in having what humans have: society, culture, philosophy, and other aspects that distinguish us from animals. This is a generalization, but monsters don't typically have these things, or at least, not in a way beyond that of animals. We can argue, rightly, that animals like dolphins and apes have a certain social structure, but these are communicated as much with body language as verbally. Any language is fairly limited compared to mankind. They don't read and write or pass down long histories. A generation today likely has no idea what was happening one hundred years ago, though this is admittedly conjecture.

None of this means we can't have an intelligent monster if we choose to, but once we start giving a monster these things, it starts moving in the direction of humanity. We may find ourselves deciding that our monster is very cool and could be more useful, so we turn it into a species. No harm in that. Dracula is a good example of a smarter monster, but while he is a vampire now, he was once human. This is also true of zombies, who are typically portrayed as relatively stupid. We can use a similar approach (the monster was once human) to explain our monster's sophistication.

Does monster automatically mean unsophisticated like an animal? In fantasy, SF, and gaming, yes. They're typically portrayed as things that can't be reasoned with when one corners us for dinner or we wander into its territory. In this sense, they're just like animals. We likely can't communicate verbally with it, either, but that's not a rule either. We can teach pets to understand what words mean, but that involves frequent time together, a reality that would make someone no longer think of the monster as such, most likely. This raises the idea of most people thinking it's a monster but one person having befriended it, which has been done with children's stories.

MONSTERS VS. ANIMALS

A major difference between monsters and animals is numbers. Just about every monster we've heard of was a "one off," meaning only one existed. The reason is the aforementioned purpose in a story—to teach a specific lesson that didn't require more of them—and because they are abnormal, which by definition means uncommon.

This is not to say we can't have more than one. Zombies and vampires are good examples, but in both cases, these originated from humans and we don't generally consider them monsters even if they're monstrous. In a film series like *Aliens*, we have what appears to be a monster but which is really an animal. Why? Numbers.

If we have more than one, can we still call it a monster? Sure, though "creature" might be a better term, but if we read the definition of that, it means animal. Does our audience care about definitions? Probably not. Either way, the existence of two or more identical monsters benefits from a good explanation, such as both of them being created at the same time as in a laboratory accident. Even then, there's no reason to say that the accident caused identical mutations. One accident could cause twenty different monsters, not twenty of one type, which are capable of reproducing and then being considered animals. Once we start multiplying them, we're going to start needing a name for them, at least, and unless they scatter, they might start developing more sentience (like society and language), sooner or later, and start becoming a species.

We needn't ever refer to our creation as a monster, but people use this term partly because there is only one. It has no name. It's an "it," as well, not a he or she, even if it appears to have a known gender. No one knows what to call it, unless it's been nearby a long time and someone gave it a nickname that stuck. In the book *Frankenstein*, the monster has no name, but because promo efforts for the movies use the monster prominently, people often think its name is Frankenstein when that's really the doctor's name.

ORIGINS

We needn't tell our audience where the monster came from originally, and in gaming it's arguably irrelevant, but the thought exercise can make the result more interesting. The first question should be whether it exists on purpose or by accident.

ACCIDENTAL MONSTERS

In worlds with magic, advanced technologies, or unexplained phenomena, the accidental route is especially viable. This is where many comic book characters originate. There are many possibilities that need little in the way of explaining how the monster came about. It encountered something and now it's a monster. That's it. No one is going to say our mutated human isn't possible.

This raises an important point—accidents happen to pre-existing entities, whether animal or a humanoid species. They don't generally cause a lifeform to spring from nonliving matter. We can do whatever we want, like having a broom become possessed of life as in *The Sorcerer's Apprentice*, but none of us regard that as a monster. It's an animate object.

This also suggests that plants can become monsters even if we don't usually refer to them that way, but "monster" implies the ability to interact and to change location, not an inanimate object rooted to the ground. After all, a monster that can't change location typically isn't particularly terrifying. We could just stay out of reach or wall it up if desired. Maybe it can move but is tied to its lair, literally or figuratively, for some reason we'd want to reveal. Then again, maybe it has telekinetic powers and can influence people over a wide area, messing with their minds so that they have hallucinations, the most important of those being hiding its true whereabouts—or tricking people into coming near enough to become food, like the sirens of Greek mythology.

The accidental route means our monster having some intelligence is more feasible, if it was once human or another sentient species. Years or even decades in the mutated state could have rendered that intelligence muted. Or the incident could've immediately rendered it dumber. Or vastly smarter.

Someone caught in an accident has one advantage— our sympathy. They're a monster now, but maybe once it was a good person with a family, one it wishes to see but is afraid to visit. It might either scare them or something worse, like feel a desire to eat them because that's what they do as a monster now, having poor impulse control. The monster may recall their past life and be hostile precisely because that old life is gone. This gives it motivation, discussed more below.

WHO CAUSED IT?

We'll need to decide who and/or what caused the accident. Readers want to know such things once one is mentioned. SF offers countless ways for this to happen, from alien weapons, physics gone awry, chemical experiments, or space phenomena. In fantasy, magic, otherworldly creatures, or other supernatural elements are likely sources.

Not all accidents just happen. Some are the result of whatever pursuit someone had, such as trying to manipulate matter or subdue forces. This is a good chance to dream up a scenario that led to the accident. We may have a story to tell as a result. Other characters crop up. Maybe our monster is the one behind the accident but blames someone else. Another option is for someone to have been purposely exposed to something that is intended to kill them but which results in a monster instead. Then there's the innocent bystander or even a hero who meant to stop an atrocity but is now a monster.

MONSTERS BY DESIGN

Some monsters might have been created on purpose, from something already alive or something inanimate. The latter suggests great power behind its creation, such as a wizard or god, both found in fantasy but often not in SF. This suggests that fantasy can get away with monsters that are farther removed from humans and animals than science fiction, where mutation of pre-existing life is more likely. But there's nothing that says technology, if it's advanced enough, can't create life from nothing.

Either way, our monster by design likely has a purpose. It's possible someone was experimenting with creating life, like Dr. Frankenstein. But that's been done, which is not to say that we can't do it, too, but we should strive for a fresh angle if we do. Maybe the monster's creation was successful and it's here for a reason, such as guarding something. Or terrorizing villages at a wizard's beckoning, which suggests story ideas. The creator should have some reason as to why they did it.

Maybe the monster is still fulfilling its purpose. Is it proud of that, or does it wish it were free of it? Is it bound somehow? Perhaps its purpose is long gone and it doesn't know what to do with itself. Perhaps its master has been destroyed and the monster is on its own now. Or the master was imprisoned and the faithful monster intends to free him. The monster may never really have a purpose at all. These monsters might experience an existential crisis like Frankenstein's monster, who is tormented by its existence and doesn't understand what it did wrong to be cast out by its creator.

This sort of monster can also elicit sympathy if desired. Slavery is still slavery. The monster can be tormented by its existence. Maybe it will even welcome death at the hands of those seeking to slay it, but maybe it fears that others want to capture it, and so it must fight back. There's always the monster that's content with being one, which is probably more likely with a monster created on purpose than with a monster created by accident (and which may remember the past or be disabled in some way that makes its existence especially hateful).

Humans have a moral and ethical code. Monsters are depicted as not having one. This helps us use them as they were often intended, as a warning about untoward behavior. But monsters may have a moral code, too, just one very different from ours, where the killing of sentient life is no big deal to them, for example. Their creator might've wanted to imbue them with certain traits, like protection of them or an item. That raises the question of how much control the creator had/has over the monster. Is the creator dissatisfied with his work? Are monster and master bound in mutual loathing but dependency? If the master is killed, will the monster die, and vice versa?

Who Caused It?

Who would create a monster on purpose? Wizards, gods, and "mad" scientists come to mind (like Dr. Frankenstein and Dr. Jekyll). So do bad people who've captured others and who want to see what happens when someone is exposed to something dangerous. It's possible that no one knows who created a given monster, meaning we don't have to mention it, but stories do well when there's some speculation about a monster's origin. Mystery is good, but not total mystery, which is why we all love clues.

Any character willingly creating monsters is likely up to no good. The creator's motivation should be understandable even if the logic behind what they've done is terrible and twisted. In fantasy, gods are a great choice because they might like creating beings for reasons never explained to the species. Or maybe they just want to keep life interesting for sentient inhabitants by creating monsters they have to deal with. SF offers many ways to expose someone to phenomenon, including viral infections from new worlds.

Monsters by Evolution

A monster can be a product of evolution, perhaps the first of its kind. In this scenario, our monster's habitat is likely to cause the resulting monster and its attributes. Evolution causes adaptation to solve a problem or take advantage of environmental factors that have usually been in place a long time. That's not to say that we can't have something happen shortly after a change in that habitat, but that's more suggestive of an accident causing the monster than evolution, which by definition takes a long time.

The X-Men took the route of evolution to explain the mutants, and though we may not consider them monsters, the non-evolved humans in the stories do. Superman has abilities bestowed by virtue of being an alien, even though those abilities are only explained as having something to do with the sun, and everyone accepts that. Our explanation can be as simple as naming the type of radiation that caused a mutation.

The changes in our monster by evolution might have no particular purpose other than to survive better than before. This can include adaptations that make it better at defeating our humanoid species. In this case, our monster will originate from an animal or species and therefore be seen as a perversion of that, much the same way a human with two heads was once considered a monster. Aside from the mutation, the monster will be similar to its original life form. Having been cast out, it might be upset with its own species.

HABITAT

Where a monster lives is important to any story involving it, even if its home is never shown. What it takes with it from there, how far away it travels, and what it takes home will affect our uses of the monster. Showing its home gives us an opportunity to characterize the monster, while avoiding doing so, or just giving hints, helps create mystery about it.

Our monster may not have a lair, but the nature of monsters in literature has typically been cautionary, meaning those living near it are supposed to learn something about themselves from the existence of this monster. We don't have to follow that, but a monster that goes away for good may prevent a population from learning anything about themselves. On the other hand, traveling monsters provide new opportunities, even across other planets.

There's no reason our monster can't have access to easier means of getting around, such as a magical device or a portal near its home which it stumbled upon. For SF, a monster with access to an interstellar ship is very useful, and we can either have that ship be the monster's lair or function like a home away from home. Possible justifications are either that the monster was on a ship when it became a monster, or that a ship landed near it and it ended up onboard, likely killing the crew after launch.

A lair can include treasure, weapons, and the remains of victims, all of those being fairly standard furnishings reminiscent of Medusa's lair from Greek mythology. The bones are more likely from two occurrences—feeding on species or animals, and/or defending itself with the resulting victims left there. This is one reason to decide on our monster's tastes. If our monster leaves dead bodies around, this says something about it, whether that it doesn't care about the smell, wants to send a message, or doesn't have a clue about disposing of bodies. It might also be unaffected by any disease this could spread.

The mystery of where one lives often occupies stories to the point of being a cliché, and yet it is such an obvious concern that it's nearly inevitable for characters to search for the lair. Rather than avoid this, make your search and discovery worthwhile. While a lair is often hard to find or reach (or escape from alive), making this impossible lessens the usefulness of our monster.

To aid this, decide what kind of evidence the monster leaves when it's away from home. Are there trails or footprints leading back? Does it cover its tracks? Are spores left behind? Does it kill and leave remains or take anything with it, particularly something (or someone) valuable and which compels action to thwart it? Is the trail it leaves a trap? Is magic (in fantasy) or special tracking equipment (in SF) needed? Does it have the ability to thwart some measures?

Knowing whether our monster is nocturnal or not will figure into any stories. Things awake and prowling at night are more intimidating, but there's no reason it can't be active during the day. The effect on a population terrorized by it becomes all encompassing, for they'd still fear it more at night, just because humans, at least, fear the dark. Our monster's enemies will have some sense of its schedule and will plan their attacks for when it's sleeping, if they know its lair. If they don't, they'll be trying to trap or otherwise attack it when it's on the prowl.

MOTIVATION

What does your monster want?

TO BE LEFT ALONE?

Isolation isn't desired by most, but if everyone thinks you're hideous or evil, you probably don't want company unless it's other monsters, which raises the question of love between monsters (whether of different kinds or not). Is the monster being hunted simply because it's been seen and is feared, or has it done something to stir up other species? Do any of our species think the monster has a right to live unmolested or does pretty much everyone want to kill it? Such conflict is good for stories and a debate on the right to life.

TO HOARD TREASURE?

This idea is often used but doesn't make that much sense because treasure is no good when we can't barter it for other things. By definition, monsters aren't engaging in commerce with a larger society; it's not like the monster is going to waltz into town and buy something. One possible explanation is that it likes shiny things, which is indicative of low intelligence. A better explanation is that a given monster happens to have valuables from killing someone and taking all their stuff, possibly indiscriminately, and having little or no idea that some of it is valuable. After all, why would it know this unless the monster was formerly part of a society and remembers this? Treasure attracts thieves, but then maybe the monster considers it a good way to lure people there so it can eat them.

FOOD?

Everyone needs to eat. The bigger our monster, the more food it requires. Large, four-legged animals like horses, deer, and bison are probably staple foods. Making it a vegetarian significantly reduces the threat to species, so you might want to avoid that, unless a salad eating monster is desired for comedic effect. If the monster just wants to eat, then survival is all it's likely after, which causes an ironic problem if it feeds on the wrong thing...

For a storyteller, the biggest reason to have monsters eat intelligent species is for the horror it creates in others. For the monsters, they may have few other options. They also might not be sophisticated or moral enough to make a distinction. Feeding on the humanoid species, or livestock can rapidly cause conflict. Most monsters are remotely located, however, so wildlife is more likely to be a staple food. Humanoid species aren't that appetizing, in reality, due to the ratio of bones to muscle/meat on us. This is why sharks spit out most people they attack; we aren't a juicy seal, for example.

SECURITY?

A monster that feels threatened is likely to attack others, especially those it believes to be encroaching on its territory. Monsters can be afraid, just as any apex predator can be. A monster could be smart enough to realize that attacking the species might bring greater numbers of them to destroy it, but it's entirely likely that a monster doesn't think that far ahead. Traditionally, monsters have a lair, which they presumably want to protect so they feel safe, but if our monster can fly or is otherwise quite mobile and a traveler, that greater freedom may give it less need of security. Then again, it might feel more vulnerable by not having a good place to hide. The idea of a monster who has recently taken up residence near a town is a good story premise.

REVENGE?

Whether our monster resulted from an accident or not, it might want revenge on its creator. Does our monster know who created it? A monster upset with life itself might just want to kill from jealousy or hatred, but it's often better in storytelling to have more interesting reasons than that. The "I'm a monster, therefore I kill" idea is stale. The monster might want revenge against the species that created it while leaving others alone. This can cause a perplexing mystery for characters. Imagine that elves caused the monster, who kills elves but leaves humans alone. The characters may not understand why at first until uncovering the backstory on this monster.

CHARACTERISTICS

PHYSICAL APPEARANCE

That monsters are hideous comes with the territory, usually, but there's no reason that has to be the case. Modern readers can consider someone or something a monster not for its appearance, but behavior. That said, a young adult audience is probably expecting a repulsive appearance. Sometimes it seems that everything ugly has already been done and that films, in particular, try to outdo each other, sometimes to the point of being unintentionally silly. The concept of beautiful monsters has also been done more recently, with anyone encountering that monster unsuspecting due to appearance, and this is sometimes an illusion. These are all valid options.

If we opt for the physically grotesque, inspiration can come from many of literature's existing beasts. Unfortunately, today's audiences have likely seen just about everything, so a monster will be made more memorable by having a rationale behind that appearance. Adding deformities or additional limbs or heads is easy and effective if not particularly imaginative, nor is merging different body parts from other animals together.

For this reason, it's suggested to figure out other aspects of our monster before working on appearance. When we get to this point, we'll already know this monster and give it physical attributes that help it achieve its motives or which derive from its origins. Justifications make the body choices more compelling, sensible, and our monster easier to standout. We face stiff competition on appearance so that we might have little chance of doing something that hasn't been done. The key to being memorable is backstory and justifications for the body.

Regardless of what we decide for appearance, having a clear idea of what our monster looks like, and the impression it creates, is important. If it looks just like humans, for example, few will think it's a monster. There must be some sort of mutation or transformation that has taken place; either that, or it is odd to begin with. Size is a simple way to make something fearful, but gigantism and dwarfism have been done before. If you go that route, I'd suggest additional reasons your monster is a monster.

A monster that results from an accident is more likely to be disproportionate in some way. One arm longer than the other, a misshapen hump, or an extra but useless limb (known as a vestigial limb) are examples. These are the reasons why humans have historically called someone with a birth defect a monster (nice of us, isn't it?). We judge by appearance, like it or not, and react with fear and revulsion to anything unusual.

SKILLS

A monster who can do unusual things is arguably more entertaining than one that's only creepy. These can be physical feats such as incredible strength, speed or endurance, the ability to regenerate severed limbs, or the power to influence minds to kill, submit, or lie to others about the monster. Whatever it is can be suggested by its appearance or we can make them a surprise to the audience or characters. Supernatural skills offer more room for being unusual and memorable. Medusa could turn people to stone. Sirens could mesmerize victims into approaching. Try to think of something that's related to the purpose the monster will have in the story and you'll do better at inventing a monster.

WHERE TO START

We can start wherever we like, but if we have an idea for a monster, we should write down everything that has already occurred to us. The template in appendix 4 can help organize our thoughts and inspire us to think of areas we haven't yet considered. We often have an appearance and behavior in mind, possibly while imagining it scaring or attacking our characters. This suggests focusing on skills and its body. Its habitat should also be considered early on, and this may be part of our initial concept; but once decided, we can determine how this impacted its body. We can round out our creation by deciding on our monster's origins before its motivations, as one typically leads to the other.

6

———◆•••◆———

CREATING PLANTS
AND ANIMALS

It takes less time to invent an animal than a humanoid species, gods, or even monsters because animals aren't as complex. Plants are even simpler. First we'll consider whether we should invent them or not. Then we'll look at specifics for each and then considerations that apply to both.

Appendices 5 and 6 are templates for creating a plant or animal respectively. They include more comments and advice, and editable Microsoft Word files that can be downloaded for free by signing up for the newsletter at http://www.artofworldbuilding.com/newsletter/

SHOULD WE CREATE
PLANTS & ANIMALS?

Creating plants or animals unique to our setting is one of the more optional world building tasks for fantasy, where no one expects it or will complain if we don't. We tend to assume a fantasy world is much like Earth, with the addition of elves, magic, and monsters, for example. We can create just a few plants or animals, tons of them, or none at all. Given that it's optional, we can benefit from thinking about why we're creating them, which is the focus of this section.

In SF that takes place exclusively on space craft, we can ignore the subject altogether unless the ship is from Earth or if we want to comment on what the crew are eating, for example. Or if they have an area similar to a greenhouse, zoo, or nature preserve for the same reasons we have parks in major cities: respite from steel, plastic, and concrete surroundings.

In SF that takes place on non-Earth planets, or ships originating from them, we can't expect the same plants and animals. Even if the world is Earth-like, the life could be very different. Something that looks like a bear at first glance might be an herbivore that makes a good pet. Details are what distinguish life forms from each other.

Vegetation doesn't need to be wildly different in basic form; there will still be trees, shrubs, and flowers, for example, but we have the option to imbue them with new properties, colors, and significance. This is fairly easy and maybe even necessary to be believable, but we don't need to invent an entire ecosystem.

Similarly, animals from another planet will still fall into broad categories like fish, amphibian, mammals, birds, and more. Since animals move and are prey and/or predator, behavior becomes an important aspect of inventing something different from an Earth analogue. For example, a horse with two more legs will strike the audience as exactly that. The appearance, size, temperament, and behavior of such a non-Earth "horse" (we'll want to call it something else) should likely be different in meaningful ways so the audience does not have that reaction. Details are how we achieve this. How to do so is discussed more in the next section.

What is our purpose with inventing this life? Do we

need an animal that's based on an Earth one but which has physical or behavioral attributes that Terrestrial ones don't? Our characters might use a horse-like animal or giant bird for travel. Maybe we need a lion that can be tamed and ridden like a horse. We might need a snake for its venom that an assassin will use. We might have a humanoid species that wears a bear pelt, except that in the absence of bears, we need a similar (but not too similar) animal. Perhaps we have a wizard who needs a rare plant for casting a deadly spell. And most common of all, we could have either a plant or animal that preys upon our humanoid species. Having a goal helps.

CREATING SOMETHING DIFFERENT

One reason to create plants and animals is that they can give our world a different look and feel. The more we create, the more pronounced this impression, especially when we link choices and behaviors of our characters to the life around them. This could be steeds that are ferocious and require great strength of will to control, but could be predators which cause travel plans to change. James Cameron did this to great effect in the movie *Avatar*.

Characters can learn hunting, attack, and defense skills based on those predators. Maybe they know what it means when a predator flees, such as when great white sharks suddenly swim away from a person in the water; it means an even bigger great white is moving in. This sort of thing is how we integrate everything. If done well, this can make our world stand out in a good way that makes audiences eager for more. The more life forms we create, the more different our world begins to feel.

HOW OFTEN THE SETTING WILL BE USED

If we'll only write one book in this setting, the extra work to create many plants and animals may not be worth it. Just do what you need for the project. Some of what we create for one world can be used in another instead, so inventing things we don't use right now is not an issue. In SF, we may have multiple worlds in a single work or across our career, so we can still just invent life forms for their own sake and figure out where to use them later. Integrating things is great, but that arguably matters more with humanoid species than plants and animals.

TIME

It takes time we may not have to create unique plants and animals, though this time investment is less than with other things in this book. We can get around this by inventing during writing, but we must watch out for creating something without much depth or impact on our work. If inventing on the fly, always make a note to add this lifeform to your files and work it out in more detail, then touch up your depiction if necessary. Integrating it with other things is a continuous process anyway.

DO OUR CREATIONS MATTER?

In the film and TV industries, having interesting plants and animals in the background is easy and fairly standard with today's special effects, and they need no more than an appearance. It's only when they affect character decisions or storylines that they achieve relevance, which is the point at which they should be mentioned in written stories. If we mention an irrelevant plant or animal in passing without some hint that it's a large cat, for example, it can be off-putting, especially if we name too many in a row.

As a case in point, in my story "The Epic of Ronyn," a character gets pelted with vegetables. I had originally named the different items he's struck with, but beta-readers commented that they had no idea what I was talking about and it took them out of the scene. I wasn't going to explain each item in the paragraph (and there was no room or reason to beforehand) because it wasn't worth it, so I replaced my list of vegetables with the word "vegetables." While not exactly descriptive, it helped the scene stay on focus.

On the other hand, "The Garden of Taria" story features a character who keeps invading someone's home and preparing a meal for himself and sometimes her, too. All of their conversations occur while food is being prepared, consumed, or cleaned up. This provided a good chance to name and very briefly describe various items, but it proved challenging to keep it to a minimum. A few choice words are recommend when writing.

For example, consider this line: "She saw a line of *yellow drops* leading from kitchen to couch, discarded *juna peels* tossed here and there along the way, the perpetrator licking the running *juices* from dirty fingers as he popped another *fruit* piece into his mouth." I added the italics to indicate the key words carefully strewn through this sentence to get across what the food is. Is this better than writing, "He ate a yellow citrus fruit called juna?" Both have their merits.

PLANTS

When creating plants, we must know their climate, which is covered in *Creating Places, (The Art of World Building, #2)*. But unless ours is an ice world, for example, it can be assumed that all climates exist somewhere, which means that we don't need to know which continents or regions our plant is found in just yet. It can be invented for a climate, and when we decide where on our world those climates exist, we'll know if it could be found there. We may want to name it after a place, or vice versa, but that's easy enough to accomplish later.

CLASSIFICATION

There are broad categories that plants fall into, but we're most likely interested in only a few.

The seedless plants include algae, liverworts, mosses, and ferns, with only mosses being something we're likely to use in our stories partly because no one thinks algae or ferns are interesting, and no one knows what a liverwort is (and it's not interesting or useful when you do). If we have sea dwelling species, algae can be more useful if there's a dangerous or useful kind that can develop.

The usefulness of moss is debatable, but it can be needed by wizards or have properties to make it deadly or otherwise cover a landscape with a color different than the green we expect on Earth. Mosses grow in damp areas and need plentiful water to reproduce. They can grow on rocks, trees, or discarded items. A special kind of moss, called sphagnum, can form floating islands found in bogs, where trees and other plants are growing in the shifting mat of clumped-together moss.

Among the plants with seeds are cycads, conifers, and flowering plants. An internet search on cycad will reveal plants that look like a palm tree, or an evergreen fern with very large leaves atop a branchless tree trunk (sometimes quite tall) and with cones in the middle of these leaves at the top. They grow slowly and live up to a thousand years, so they could be admired by a long living, humanoid species. They are in tropical and subtropical climates. These large cones can be imagined to contain useful material in them and to have predators who desire them.

A conifer also has cones but prefers colder climates and often forms enormous forests. Conifers include pines, cedars, Douglas-firs, junipers, redwoods, spruces, and more. Most are trees but some are shrubs. Their conical shape helps them shed snow and their wood is soft.

Then there are the flowering plants that dominate temperate climates; unless you live somewhere always cold or hot, this is what you see when you look out the window, and as such, these are the most common plants you'll be inventing. These include not only flowers, shrubs, and vines but trees like the oak, maple, elm, aspen, and birch.

Regarding trees, the deciduous variety lose their leaves in autumn while the evergreens lose them continuously all year in such a way as to appear, by contrast, that they never lose their leaves, hence the name.

What does this all mean to a world builder? Not much other than having a better understanding of what we probably want to invent: mosses, conifers, and flowering plants, with algae and cycads bringing up the rear.

LIFECYCLE

While trees live decades, plants like flowers don't. This matters because we can make a plant rare by shortening its lifecycle according to established (or invented) lifecycles. And rare plants are considered more potent in spells.

Some plants are annuals. This means the plant's lifecycle is one season before it dies. If we want a petunia (an annual) in the same spot in our garden every year, be prepared to plant new ones annually. A biennial, less common on Earth, lives two years, producing foliage in one year and flowers the next; many are vegetables, producing food one year and leaving seeds the next. A plant that lives longer than two years is a perennial and usually drops all leaves by winter before returning in spring. Most vines are perennials, remaining in place year after year but flowering at certain times of the year.

A bulb is a short stem that has roots growing from one side and an undeveloped shoot from the other, from where the stem eventually grows. They go through stages, the interesting one for us being that if a bulb is dug up before the foliage stage is complete (the flowers aren't out), it won't bloom the following year but will in subsequent years; more importantly, if dug up after the foliage stage is complete, it can be stored for four months for planting elsewhere. Imagine a dangerous/useful plant that's a bulb and grows somewhere unique but can be harvested and transported and replanted elsewhere.

ANIMALS

While there are many types of animals we could create, some are more likely candidates than others. To get started, knowing how they're classified might give us ideas.

CLASSIFICATION

Animals are either invertebrates or vertebrates; i.e., spineless or not. The distinction has no other significance.

Invertebrates, which make up 97% of animals, include worms, sea urchins, jellyfish, snails, arachnids (spiders, scorpions), crustaceans (lobster, crab), corals, and insects. On Earth, they tend to be smaller than vertebrates, but Jabba the Hutt from *Star Wars* was a huge worm, and the giant spider from *The Lord of the Rings* is infamous. Our characters are unlikely to use invertebrates for domestication, sport, guards, or transportation unless we make them enormous, so our use of them is limited, but they can be food, pets, and used for materials. These purposes will be discussed in the next section. Swarms of such small animals, like insects, can pose a problem, and we can invent a swarm that takes place at given intervals (as with cicada) that people prepare for, for example. Imagine that with giant insects.

Vertebrates include the animals you probably thought of when starting this chapter: amphibians, birds, fish, mammals, and reptiles.

AMPHIBIANS

Amphibians include frogs, toads, and salamanders, and require water to breed, laying larva that metamorphose into the adult form. They are capable of living on land or underwater but need moist habitats to keep their skin damp. They can acquire air through their skins to assist their lungs, with a few having no lungs at all; this allows them to remain submerged indefinitely. They are typically small but one extinct species on Earth was up to thirty feet. Being coldblooded, they rely on environment to regulate body temperature and have slow metabolism, meaning they require less food and expend less energy. Their tongues are muscular and can often protrude surprisingly far, being coiled up when not in use.

Some species have skin glands that secrete poison, whereas some secretions just make them taste bad so they'll be spit out instead of consumed. Some are lethal to humanoids and this is a good reason to invent some amphibians for our world, for use as poisons. The poisonous ones are often brightly colored as a warning and are more likely to actively search for prey, their appearance warning away predators. The camouflaging amphibians ambush prey.

Frogs can be venomous, too. The difference between venom and poison isn't well understood by lay people, but venom must be injected into the body. This typically means being stung, bitten, or stabbed. By contrast, poisonous animals can merely be touched and are relatively passive. Venom is typically for both offense and defense while poison is for defense.

Frogs and toads appear similar except the former has smooth skin and the latter warty; both have no tail, long folding legs, and big eyes. Salamanders look more like lizards, being low, flat, and possessing a tail. All have four legs, webbed toes, and no claws. Frogs and toads have excellent hearing. They periodically shed skin in one piece and sometimes eat it (yummy).

Virtually all amphibians are predators who hunt by sight and swallow prey whole, dining on small, slow moving insects and only chewing a little to subdue their meal. Holding still is how potential victims avoid being detected and eaten, but some amphibians hunt by smell and may be able to locate prey that doesn't have a scent, even in the dark or when it's not moving. Many amphibians are nocturnal and hide during the day.

While they are seldom seen (unless you invent large ones), amphibians are heard quite often during mating season, but their calls are fatiguing to themselves and could draw predators, in addition to attracting females. A deeper voice typically means a bigger amphibian. Frogs can actually scream when attacked and their vocalization can be aggressive to ward off competition. Some amphibians are territorial about sites for breeding, shelter, or food, and physically attack if necessary. Like reptiles, some salamanders can detach their tail if a predator has them by the tail, and regrow it.

BIRDS

There's a tendency to overlook birds during world building and storytelling, probably because they have limited use to us except as food or symbols (like associating a dove with peace). Birds consume food smaller than them, so unless we have giant birds, they'll be keeping clear of our species unless they've been domesticated and used like carrier pigeons, for example, or as pets, as in the parrot. Birds of prey like hawks can be used as hunters, possibly bringing our adventurers small game like rabbits or fish for dinner. Bird eggs are among the more useful aspects, but then what's different about our bird's eggs that we can't get from a run of the mill chicken, for example?

As with all animals, when deciding to invent a bird, consider our purpose and those of our characters. We may find there's little reason to invent one that isn't an analogue; we can just combine aspects of different birds, like plumage, behavior, trainability, and prevalence, and slap a different name on them and be good to go.

Migration is one of the characteristics of a world that

might be more worthwhile to consider. Not all birds migrate, but land birds can migrate 1600 miles and shorebirds up to 2500 miles, with the longest distance for one species being 6300 miles. Some species don't necessarily return the next year, based on food availability (if that's the driving force behind migration, as breeding is the other big motive). It isn't just the carrier pigeon that can return to a specific place, as most birds can navigate incredible distances and return home.

Some species flock for safety in numbers, especially in forests where predators are harder to detect, and more eyes offer more chances to warn each other. Some birds also cooperate with other animals, such as sea-diving birds that take advantage of bait balls of fish; this happens when animals like dolphins herd small fish to the surface for themselves to eat, helping out the birds, too.

For general characteristics we might not be familiar with, most birds are diurnal but some operate at night, during twilight, or when tides are appropriate for feeding if they're a bird that wades in coastal waters. Some birds are more intelligent than most other animals, which could be interesting when combined with ferocity and large size. In contrast to reptiles and amphibians, birds rapidly digest food so they can fly again; they have no teeth and swallow most things whole. On isolated islands, birds may become flightless due to a lack of predators.

Not all birds create a nest for eggs but generally hide them from predators if so. Incubation is from ten to eighty days and in many species is only once a year, with from one to nearly a dozen eggs. This is useful to know if we're using enormous birds as in *The Lord of the Rings* because there would theoretically be a demand for such huge eggs.

FISH AND OTHER AQUATIC LIFE

Fish are aquatic animals that have fins and gills and are cold-blooded, their body temperatures affected by environment. This includes eels, actual fish, lampreys, rays, and sharks, but not some animals that have the word "fish" in their name, like jellyfish and starfish. Technically it excludes dolphin and whales, which are mammals. Some can breathe air just like us and can survive several days without suffocating. Fish may not hear well and instead depend on sensing motion, but they have excellent color vision, taste, and smell. A number of small fish have developed the ability to glide through the air for over a hundred feet, typically to evade predators.

Some fish form schools or shoals, which are slightly different. In a school, fish move at the same speed and direction, being tightly synchronized as if of one mind. By contrast, shoals are more loosely organized, the fish independent but staying close. Like birds, they are sometimes assigned religious symbolism, which we can leverage. For example, if there was once a drought on land and fish had allowed people to survive, they might be revered.

As world builders, our primary use for fish is as food during dining scenes unless we want one to threaten humanoid species that enter the water or sail upon it. People can be stung, paralyzed, poisoned, and outright killed by sea life, whether immediately or in time. We can have someone meet their end by drowning, by being swallowed whole, or most dramatically, by being bitten to death. Piranha, sharks, and other animals with significant teeth are good models for threatening sea life.

Only the largest marine life is likely to threaten or destroy a ship-of-the-line, but giant squid and octopus have been done. You'll want to invent something unique, either a single large creature or a coordinated group of smaller ones. If we invent some unusually smart sea life, maybe they'll have another agenda or just be attracted to pretty things, like those armored knights seen upon deck. This comes close to inventing a monster (see chapter five).

MAMMALS

Mammals are the largest and smartest animals, generally, though this can be different on our world. Most have four legs, though some have adaptations extreme enough that we may not realize they're a mammal, such as whales and dolphins.

Other sea mammals include otters, polar bears, and seals, and while some aquatic mammals can survive outside of water, others will die. If inventing one, this is something we must decide on. All of them depend on the sea for food and can submerge far longer than humans. Many must come on land to breed. Either blubber, large size, or waterproof fur can be used to retain heat. Large animals use their weight to stay down where their food is (on the bottom) while lighter animals have food that is more likely to be nearer the surface. Habitat is either open sea or coastal, with the latter including kelp beds, beaches, reefs, and even rocky cliffs. Sea mammals are hunted not only for food and fur but a substance like spermaceti, which is used to make wax. These give us product ideas.

Other mammals have developed aerial locomotion. Cats have a limited ability to essentially parachute themselves to slow their fall. Tree-dwelling animals can glide between tall trees that are spaced far apart. Bats can outright fly. These traits can be used in our work.

Living in trees poses challenges that cause adaptations, which include far better balance and ability to grip a vertical surface to prevent pitching backwards or slippage. Gaps between branches must be overcome by reaching between, jumping, or gliding. Longer limbs, claws, and a prehensile tail (i.e., one that can grab things) aid these.

Walking is a distinguishing trait that comes in three types. Primates (including humans) and apes are among those with plantigrade locomotion, meaning the toes and metatarsal bones (those between toe and arch) are on the ground, along with the heel. The disadvantage is speed, caused partly by shorter, thicker legs. The advantage is being more weight bearing. Digitigrade animals like cats and dogs walk on their toes and are faster and quieter as a result. Then there's ungulate locomotion, meaning walking on the tips of the toes, which sounds painful to us, but these animals have a hoof that is perpetually growing and wearing down like our nails; these animals are usually herbivores, are faster, and often have antlers (on males).

Most mammals give live birth and nurse with milk, but a few lay eggs. Communal raising of young is the norm with pack animals in particular, unlike with non-mammals. Mammals are warm-blooded, meaning the body regulates temperature instead of relying upon ambient air or water to do so; the ability has limits, which is why mammals can die from heat stroke or hypothermia. Being warm-blooded causes higher metabolism and therefore greater need for food. Mammals can replace a tooth once or never, but we could always decide that our mammal can replace teeth every time one is lost, like sharks.

Lastly, mammals are used for food, leather, wool, experiments, pets, transportation, and entertainment, discussed in a subsequent section of this chapter.

REPTILES

Reptiles include turtles, crocodiles, snakes, and lizards. They either have four legs or none. Cold-blooded, they cannot control body heat without environmental help; while some have adapted to extreme temperatures, most stay in water or seek sun or shade as needed. A slow metabolism means less food is needed than for a mammal of the same size (as much as ninety percent less), and some can go a half year without food, though this means they aren't moving much; movement burns energy that must be replaced with a meal. Reptiles can dominate areas with little food, because there isn't enough to sustain birds and mammals. All of this also means reptiles don't do long chases and have a sit-and-wait strategy as predators, but this doesn't have to be true of ones we invent. Some small reptiles can glide through the air.

All Earth reptiles have lungs, but some have permeable skin, too, suggesting we can create a reptile without lungs if desired. Reptiles have watertight, horny skin/scales so they can live on land, unlike amphibians, but it isn't thick like mammals and can't be used for leather except in decorative fashion (as opposed to for protection or clothing). Most are carnivores or eat insects, but herbivores exist. Some reptiles consume rocks to help with digestion; such a stone is called a gastrolith. Reptiles are less intelligent than mammals and birds due to small brain size, but we can invent more intelligent and therefore more frightening ones. Most are diurnal (i.e., active during the day) but some that operate at night have a kind of thermal sight that we can make more extreme and useful, especially if we invent a humanoid species that's reptilian.

Reptiles usually produce sexually but some are asexual (where's the fun in that?). Genitals are stored within the body. Some do live birth while others lay hard or leathery eggs that almost immediately hatch.

Smaller reptiles rely on avoidance to not become a meal of birds or other reptiles. As such, they hide within underbrush and can often camouflage themselves, whether basic skin color does this or they can change it; the ability to lie still for long periods aids this. If unable to flee, they may hiss or make noise, like the rattlesnake; others make themselves appear bigger, like the cobra. Some are brightly colored to indicate they are venomous. Some actually play dead. Others can detach their tail and run away, the tail still wiggling for up to twenty minutes to distract their predator from their fleeing; some of these tails are brightly colored to encourage an attack there, but regardless, the tails grow back but not usually to the same length, and may be discolored compared to the original.

PURPOSE

Beyond our purpose in inventing a plant or animal, we can think about how they are used by our world's inhabitants. Food is an obvious way, and some food will have cultural or religious ideas associated with them; some items might be forbidden or ritually slaughtered first, though we'll want a rationale for such decisions, such as deciding an animal offended a god. Imagine a deity who was once on an important mission that became delayed by a herd of animals, or by a forest of a given tree type; now this is seen as the reason the god failed to achieve something. The resulting religion could forbid use of the item, either by the god's decree or not.

PLANTS

Plants are used in many ways that we can adopt when inventing one. The obvious example, besides creating oxygen, is for food, but there's also decoration, medicine, building materials, toys, clothing, tools, fuel, and everyday items like pencils and paper. Chemical processes often require or benefit from plants, such as fermenting beer or brewing coffee. Many of these aren't glamorous or of much interest to an audience, but when doing research on analogues, you'll learn what any given plant is typically used for and can leverage the information.

Often, not every part of a plant has the properties that make it special. The leaves can be deadly while the stem or seeds are not. When crafting a plant, decide which part makes it valuable and if anything must be done to that part for it to acquire its purpose. Leaves might need to be crushed. The pulp might need to be boiled.

DECORATION

Decoration is a useful subject if we decide that people in a given culture have assigned certain properties to a flower, for example, and assume that a female wearing one in her hair is revealing something about herself to others. Garlands of a given flower type can be used at ceremonies, such as burial or graduation. These uses require less invention of details because an audience will accept them as cultural and having little basis.

FOOD

Plants offer a good opportunity to have our characters and story affected by interesting foods. They can be poisonous, addictive, a bland staple for adventurers, freely found in the wild, or a cultural or religious expectation to serve or consume at certain moments. A culture clash can result for traveling characters. Even if we don't use plants in a significant way, they can still be briefly mentioned during any scene involving their consumption.

MEDICINAL

Invented medicinal plants are great for healing or poisoning our characters or for use in spells. We need no explanation for why a plant has these properties because audiences don't expect one, though in a more scientific world or story, one will help. Plants with supernatural properties are often said to grow near something like a special spring or dark place. The habitat can be the reason the plant acquires unique properties—or even loses them if away for too long, such as once plucked. Are the plants themselves supernatural?

ANIMALS

As with plants, humanoid species use animals in many ways, including as food, pets, transportation, entertainment/sport, guards, domestic work, and for materials such as hides, bones, and even fluids. Other humanoid species can also be used for these things, as distasteful as humans usually find the subject. We can use Earth animals or invent our own, which can be inspired by a desire to do something new or have an Earth animal do things one on Earth doesn't do. Maybe the only horses available for riding are similar but much harder to control or train. Or maybe they are carnivores and sometimes eat their riders. Maybe we can ride one but never with a saddle. Each of these might pose a problem for characters, adding dynamics to a story. We'd probably want to call this something other than a horse, changing physical attributes while we're at it.

DOMESTICATION

Domestic work like pulling wagons isn't very thrilling, but such animals are likely to be more commonly experienced by characters in urban settings. They can be mentioned during scenes directly involving them or just in passing as they contribute to smells, filth, and other delights only animals can add to life. In SF, machines may have replaced such uses, at least for those wealthy enough to afford them. World-hopping characters may visit a world without such technology and have an inability to deal with animals like this, struggling to ride them, for example.

ENTERTAINMENT/SPORT

Humans often use animals for sport, whether hunting them, fighting them against each other, or racing them against each other. Some see animals as trophies and the hunt a sign of their virility. This can be used to characterize our characters. Inventing unique attributes for an animal can make this conquest worthwhile. While making it faster, more ferocious, or just rare is good, consider granting abilities like teleportation, hiding/disguising of its tracks, or greater intelligence and cunning than we expect of Earth animals. The name of such an animal can become a nickname for a character.

FOOD

Animals used as food are either hunted or kept in a pasture. The former is a more entertaining use in our work and requires preparation, skill, knowledge, and the right tools. This also exposes our characters to risk if the animal can fight back. Even if they can't, hunting typically means the wild, where other animals, species, monsters, and even supernatural phenomenon could impact the hunt. Dinner scenes can be spiced up with brief mention of the taste, feel, and desirability of what's being consumed. Animals can also produce eggs, milk or other fluids that others imbibe.

Animals kept in a pasture or pen are usually more docile, but not always; think of a bull. They can be docile until approached or threatened. They can also go wild if a predator comes near, howling with fear, which can aid a scene in which characters hear a bellowing animal and realize a threat to it—and them—is encroaching.

Ferocious animals are usually not considered food on Earth because the dangers they pose aren't worth the trouble, but maybe our characters have no choice or enjoy the challenge, even considering the eating of a docile animal a weakness, while the eating of something aggressive is strength; if that's the case, they probably want to hunt it, too. Such a scenario can suggest a cowardly character who dines on this beast to appear strong, but loses others' esteem when it is revealed he hasn't hunted them, but eats caged ones. This is one way we can use such animals.

GUARDS

Invented animals that can guard something are a staple of fantasy in particular. Ferocity, obedience, and difficulty killing are the usual requirements, but it can help to decide what this animal is like in the wild, too. What does it eat? It's almost certainly a carnivore that might pose a threat of eating interlopers; an herbivore is less frightening, and audiences are expecting us to out-do each other. Is this animal trained to perform its duty (more reliable) or is it chained up and ferocious enough to just attack anything that comes too close?

MATERIALS

Whether it is bone, hide, teeth and claws, or secretions, animals are often harvested for what they can be turned into. This includes trophies, decorations like jewelry, and clothing. Horns and spines can become weapons. Some whales are harvested to make candles from wax in their heads. In a technological society, the processing for this can result in a larger number of products than the lower tech level found in most fantasy. Consider what our animal gets turned into: soap, ink, paint, cosmetics, poison, oil, wax, wool, leather, and otherworldly things that fantasy and SF can allow, such as materials for spells and chemicals used for war or peace; the same is true of plants.

PETS

Pets are another common use for animals, especially in urban areas, but the subject is generally overlooked in both fantasy and SF. A scene inside anyone's home can include mention of a pet coming, going, or being passed. Films, TV shows, or video games can also show these in passing. Then there's the areas where it's fed, poops, sleeps, or is caged if dangerous. Some pets can travel well like dogs, while others stay at home like cats. Pets offer a chance to humanize and characterize people, though it's overly simplified to say that a vicious killer has a dangerous animal when he might just have a cuddly pet.

TRANSPORTATION

New steeds are an ideal animal to create. They can have advantages and disadvantages that Earth equivalents don't; modifying an analogue to achieve a specific purpose is a good way to start. Some will be lumbering, slow pack animals pulling wagons or just heavily loaded, while others can be faster and holding little more than a rider and his supplies. Flying steeds require creative license (something that big can't really get off the ground with riders, but no one really cares) and offer aerial threats if we've taken the time to invent them. They also pose a problem for our characters, who might be unable to take everything with them, causing a potentially painful choice for what to leave behind. They need to land sooner or later, too, and this exposes characters to risk, regardless of whether they've scouted first or not, for anything could've seen them in the sky and pursued on the ground, waiting for them to land; this would be a great reason to only land at night, after many miles of not being seen.

WHERE TO START

ANALOGUES

Inventing an animal or plant is easier if we base it on one or more Earth equivalents, of which tens of thousands exist. Analogues free us from becoming experts in botany, for example, because our lifeform has details that largely match an Earth life. By contrast, inventing from scratch means needing to understand more about what defines a lifeform type, though this chapter provided enough high level details for us to do so. Generally, we'll want to portray our inventions to an audience in simple, non-technical terms unless the details are required, as in the case of an actual botanist trying to create a serum from something to cure a disease, for example.

Remember the rule of three when using an analogue: make at least three changes. Some items to alter are coloring, the number of appendages, whether an animal is trainable or not, and how the life form can be used by our humans and species (if at all). We can borrow traits from other things, like inventing cats who obey like dogs.

Be aware that many Earth lifeforms are different than we might expect. For example, in America we're used to only seeing red tomatoes. We could create yellow ones, thinking we're being different, when yellow tomatoes already exist here. Cats can actually be highly trained. We may be accustomed to seeing something portrayed a certain way when that thing is more complex or varied than we realize.

Research will often surprise us and it's worth doing for our inventions and even personal enrichment, if you care about such things. Google any plant or animal that you want to start with and read about it, making a list of interesting attributes or things that could be mentioned when writing. The details can surprise us, and when we use those details, altered or not, to introduce our plant or animal, it's more engaging. Consider this example: "A large, four-legged, herbivore with huge tusks, they mostly graze or eat leaves and other plants. Their tusks are prized. They can be tamed and are often used as pack animals, either carrying the load or pulling it." That gets us thinking and picturing it far more than if we just said "elephant."

CREATING A LIST OF ANIMALS AND PLANTS

There are so many things we could create that it's advantageous to have a categorized list of possibilities to decide on. Start with analogues in each class. Below is a small list of staples we might want to invent, using the rule of three to make each different from its source:

Mammals: boar, deer, bear, cow, goat
Sea life: shark, whale, ray, plain fish, flying fish, dolphin
Lizards: snake, crocodile
Birds: vulture, pigeon, falcon
Flowers: rose, nightshade, lily
Trees: oak, weeping willow, pine, maple
Vegetables: corn, tomato, potato
Other Plants: wheat, rice

CREATING A PRODUCTS LIST

Another approach is to make a list of products our characters might need or use and then determine their plant or animal source. Goats are used for cheese, for example. Potatoes make chips and fries. Wheat makes beer and bread. Grapes make wine. Trees are turned into all sorts of products and have typical uses depending on the tree. Research an oak tree and how it's used (and why), and then give it some different properties and similar uses. We can write something like, "He dipped the bird-name quill into the sea-life-name ink and signed his name."

7

———•••———

CREATING UNDEAD

In a book called *Creating Life*, a chapter on creating undead might seem out of place, but if it's still moving, we can consider it alive enough. A multitude of undead types already exist for our use, with most being public domain. These include vampires, zombies, ghosts, skeletons, and more. Most of them are excellent ideas that, just like elves, dwarves, and dragons, have stood the test of time. No one will roll their eyes if we use them.

SHOULD YOU CREATE UNDEAD?

The first question we must ask ourselves is whether we should create our own undead. And the answer to that is—probably not. Not unless we have a good reason or an idea that is substantially different. Most basic versions of undead already exist, leaving little room for new ones that aren't rehashed old ideas with minor twists. If we create immortal bloodsuckers that burn to ash in direct sunlight and have superhuman strength and senses, and we call them something besides vampires, people will call us out.

Conversely, there's a limit on how much we can change something and still use the original name. This is a judgment call. The first consideration is, how quickly does the way we describe and use it invoke memories of the undead we used for inspiration? The sooner it happens, the more we just call it what it is. We want to avoid the "Oh, it's just a vampire with this and that added or removed" reaction.

The second factor is whether the changes we've made substantially alter the nature of the source. If our creation is a vampire but doesn't drink blood, we've changed something too fundamental to call it a vampire. Some will disagree with this and say authors can do whatever we want, and while this is sort of true, there are expectations that can be defied and ones that shouldn't be. If changing something fundamental, just change it even more and invent a name.

THE MIND

This is an academic debate, but in death, does the mind go with the soul or remain with the body? Depending on our point of view, this can be used to determine the mental faculties of our undead. For example, we assume that if the soul goes to an afterlife, the mind goes with it and is fully intact. This would suggest that ghosts generally have their minds, whether those minds are impaired by their present state or not. Corporeal undead that have a soul would also have a mind, in theory.

But what about corporeal undead that have no soul in the body? Is that undead largely mindless? About as intelligent as an animal? It's something to consider if creating undead, or at least use as a rationalization point. It can help us determine what our undead is capable of.

Either way, we can introduce mental impairment of any kind so that our undead is "not right in the head."

Such impairment includes denial of death. This might seem odd with a spirit. After all, a spirit doesn't have a body, so how can they not realize they're dead? Yet there are many ghost stories that include this idea. In such a case, the spirit is often behaving as if it's alive, going about its usual business, such as housework or even rocking a baby's crib. If confronted with the truth of their demise, these spirits can experience the usual wrath that even the living exhibit when an unpleasant truth is thrust upon them. The trouble with inventing this type of spirit is that we're not really inventing it—it's a standard ghost.

A generally accepted idea for undead is that they're tormented. We speak of "rest in peace" and other phrases about the dead, the connotation being that anyone not lying still must necessarily be upset about that fact. Even Dracula, for all his seeming enjoyment of his state, is shown as tormented when no one is looking. If life is an ideal state and death is the worst we expect, then being undead is an unexpected half-life with even less of a training manual on what to do. Torment can be emotional or mental in origin but affects both. The degree to which our undead is upset about its state may help determine its goals and traits, discussed in this chapter.

CLASSIFICATION

SENTIENT LIFE

The first choice to make with undead is whether they have a body or not. If so, the term undead is often used, as it implies a body that it is animated once again. If there's no body, it's a spirit, which is a slightly more generic term than ghost. That's not a rule, but I'm going with the following terms in this chapter:

1. Spirits—it has no body
2. Corporeal—it has a body, with or without a soul in it

3. Undead—a generic word meaning both or either of the above

SPIRITUAL UNDEAD

The existence of a soul is debatable and outside the scope of this book, but without one, we don't have spiritual undead. We may find it difficult to invent one that hasn't been done before partly because, without a body, our options are more limited than with corporeal undead, who can touch and affect the world.

One way around this is to decide that our spirit can interact with the physical world anyway, possibly with limitations. Perhaps they can only do so for short periods or under the right conditions. Maybe they become vulnerable while doing so, or afterwards for a time. Maybe the spirits that can pass through objects (an advantage) can't move them (a disadvantage), or the reverse, it can't pass through objects but can move them. Inventing such details is one way to create something unique.

Where is the spirit's body? This could be used for motivation or characterization. A popular idea is that destroying the body eliminates the spirit, which may know this and hide or protect its remains. The spirit might wish to reanimate the body. It might be unhappy with where the body lies, such as an improper burial, or if it's being used as a trophy. These speak to motivation, covered later, but the corpse may be irrelevant.

For more details, see the section under "traits."

CORPOREAL UNDEAD

Corporeal undead come in two varieties—those with a soul and those without. There may not be much difference at first glance. In the above section about the mind, if we accept the premise that the mind goes with the soul, then a soulless corpse might be mentally deficient. Perhaps this explains depictions of zombies, though I don't recall anyone explicitly stating they have no soul. The brain (not the same as the mind) is technically what allows for control of the body and it can be assumed to be impaired due to lack of blood supply, at the least, so this can be another explanation for traits. It's all make believe, but our willing suspension of disbelief is aided by something plausible.

The existence of the body gives us more options than a spirit. Our undead could have super senses instead of worse ones, leading to an altered personality or character. For example, an undead with super hearing might be able to learn things they otherwise couldn't by overhearing conversations not meant for their ears. The new knowledge might give them a feeling of power that might've been denied them in life. Consider how this might affect their minds, emotions, and motivations.

Being dead means a loss of body function, but this depends on our creation. In many recent works, vampires show heightened senses and don't appear dead, so much so that one can question whether these are really vampires or super human people who can't really be killed except by specific means like sunlight. We've even seen vampires having babies. The point is that we can decide on undead that are a vision of health, a rotting corpse, or just a skeleton. There are no limits, but each offers a very different experience for the undead and anyone encountering them.

In theory, a skeleton should be unable to move at all, having no muscles or anything else needed for locomotion, not to mention a brain to control limbs. This is largely true of a decaying corpse, as well, but at least the decay suggests movement is only hampered. Without the supernatural or technology to allow locomotion and more, corporeal undead are more nonsensical than spirits, so if we have a world without either, they may not make sense, not that anyone's stopping us from doing it anyway.

We might think that a skeleton implies that death occurred longer ago than with a partially decomposed or preserved body, but this is not true. The rate of decomposition depends on many factors, including exposure to air, water, or earth, and the level of aridity and even water in soil. A skeleton could be a decade old while a body preserved under the right conditions could be a thousand years old, whether this preservation was intentional or inadvertent. For some interesting if gross reading (not for the faint of heart), read this article: http://www.memorialpages.co.uk/articles/decomposition.php

NON-SENTIENT LIFE

PLANTS

Undead plants? Sure, why not? We think of undead as having previously had a mind and soul (i.e., being sentient), neither of which apply here, but anything that's alive can die. And come back to life while not quite being the same. The subject is underutilized in fiction, maybe for good reasons.

Without a soul, spiritual undead plants are not an option, leaving only corporeal undead plants. Plants aren't mobile, typically, and are therefore even easier to avoid than the slow moving zombies of yesteryear. This makes plants not particularly frightening. We also assume they can't grow, being dead, so they can't even extend their range.

If we want undead plants that terrify, a predatory and mobile one has better options once dead and back to life. If there are walking and talking plants similar to the Ents of *The Lord of The Rings*, our options increase considerably. Wouldn't it be interesting for plants to not lose attributes as undead, but gain them instead? What if one became sentient?

ANIMALS

We see undead animals less often than humanoids, making this a ripe area for originality. If undead humanoids have reduced capabilities, animals might, too, but authors have often given undead animals augmented ones instead. What if it's smarter now, even able to speak? The supernatural can grant this without explanation, as can technology. Great strength or speed are clichés but are done to make them more formidable, which could now be done with intelligence, too. An undead animal can continue with a behavior from life even if it's no longer needed, such as eating or hunting. The obvious thing here is for an appetite that's now sinister, such as preying on people. This can include swarms of insects who now do this and infect the living, who might in turn become undead.

NUMBERS

How many of this undead type exist? Is there only one? Is that because it just started existing yesterday and there hasn't been time for more yet, or because whatever caused it was a one-time phenomenon? Maybe someone created it on purpose and the creator's now dead, leaving no one who knows how the undead creature was created. We'll look more into origins next, but the issue of population count is tied to origins.

It might be possible for powerful wizards or those with certain technology to turn people into this kind of undead when desired. This is a good source of indefinite numbers when we need them for our work. The living can be instantly turned into one or killed and brought back. And the dead can be raised, requiring access to them first.

Can our undead replicate itself via a bite? This could mean a larger population, and a somewhat naturally occurring issue (compared to someone creating more on purpose), but in a limited geographic area, unless travel is unusually easy for the undead. Do these new undead have any allegiance to their creator? This has been taken to extremes in some vampire lore where killing the creators kills everyone they created.

PREREQUISITES AND PREVENTION

Is there a prerequisite of some kind before something becomes a specific type of undead? Maybe any kind of person can be turned into this or only those people previously in hell or in heaven. We can decide they must have been buried in the earth, or not buried, or buried poorly, even cremated. Maybe they must've been sent floating down a river on a funeral barge, or jettisoned into space with not even a space suit on. Tying their origins to burial (or lack thereof) helps create something memorable.

Did the living or dead have to experience one thing or another to make them susceptible to this fate? This could be mundane, such as only sailors becoming those undead aboard a ghostly ship. Or a wizard in life becoming an undead capable of performing magic; one would assume that those without magic talent in life don't have it in death, but anything's fair game. What if someone had the talent but refused to use it until undead, when they're compelled to use it "for survival," by angst, or at the behest of the one who raised them?

Are there any people protected from such a fate by life or death practices? A priest comes to mind. If being turned into this undead is common, maybe people are buried in a way to prevent it, such as the head, feet, or hands being cut off. There's a custom to add to our species. It could be simpler and less gruesome than this, such as being buried with a religious item or something known to repel this fate; think of garlic and vampires.

TIME DEAD

How long was our undead not living before becoming undead? This affects appearance at the least, and possibly the mind. The latter is more affected if our world has an afterlife that this character has been wrenched back from. This sort of thing would be traumatizing, one would assume. Imagine the serenity they were enjoying. Or the horror they've escaped, for now. Having crafted an afterlife would help us here; see *Cultures and Beyond (The Art of World Building, #3)*.

In the case of vampires, the living die for a few seconds before becoming undead, which accounts for their lack of decay. They've essentially gone from alive straight to undead. Still, by definition, all undead must have been dead for at least a second, even if that renders the transition so nearly instantaneous as to be a moot point.

ORIGINS

Knowing the origins of undead is often a basic part of their identity and a good way to distinguish ours from what's come before. A good story excites the imagination. In this case, we're talking about an undead who wasn't caused by the bite of another undead, for example, but an original undead of this type.

ACCIDENTAL UNDEAD

As with monsters, undead can be created by any number of accidents, whether natural, supernatural, or technological. This might be the most common cause because few people want undead to exist *and* have the ability to go around creating them. Undead created accidentally are likely to be few in number unless a large-scale event created many of them at once. How many accidents produce the same results? If we want many spirits that are the same, and in the same area, a large accident is one way to justify that; historically, our depictions of spirits have a tendency to show them as largely solitary. A type of spirit that works in groups could be a novel approach.

We might decide that there are certain types of phenomenon that are known to create specific types of undead. If those phenomena are rare but still somewhat widespread, the resulting undead can be as well. What if someone has harnessed that phenomenon and can unleash it on purpose? That could make this undead type more common; this works for monster creation as well.

UNDEAD BY DESIGN

It's safe to say that anyone who purposely creates undead is up to no good. Our perpetrator might be able to control the result. If so, we can decide who wants to do this and why, then figure out the resulting undead attributes, or do this in reverse. Once someone has created one, they don't necessarily need to continue doing so for them to propagate. Instead, the undead may have the ability to create more of themselves, making them widespread despite having a single, original source.

If our perpetrator cannot control the resulting undead, he might be unhappy with the result. Did he try to destroy it? Chase it away? Did it retaliate and kill or wound him? Or best of all, turn him into one, too, possibly under its control?

Does the creator have control over his undead? Do they obey? Chafe at this? Or do they seemingly like it? Are they crafty enough to pretend to obey only to look for an opportunity to attack him? How does he control them? A device? A spell that's still in effect and can be nullified by a zone where magic doesn't work anymore? Or did the means used to create them make his control a given?

GOALS

Even the undead want *something*.

UNFINISHED BUSINESS

It's traditionally said that spirits stick around to finish an important task or protect someone or something.

This might be more of a character issue than one about an undead type, unless the latter always has the same goal that is apparent in behavior. Perhaps their appearance and behavior are often the same so that when taken together, the undead type is more identifiable. However, this is a basic idea about ghosts and is nothing new. We'll have to combine this with more unique issues to achieve something unique.

With unfinished business, two undead are unlikely to have the same tasks in mind unless they were created at the same moment and want retribution, for example. Two independently created undead might go about a similar goal in ways so different that this cannot be used to identify them. Revenge via murder will depend so much on their intended victim that the lack of patterns would make it harder to identify this undead as a given type.

REGAINING LIFE

Being undead might offer someone a chance at returning to life. Logically, a spirit needs a new body to inhabit. Getting back the old one won't do much good if it's still dead and decayed, and yet you'll find no shortage of stories where that exact thing happens and the body is magically (literally) restored. Technology can also be used to that effect. People don't seem to question this, but maybe creators should. Decide whether body restoration is possible. If not, our spirit can forget about its own body. Either way we have some options, and so does our spirit. These can help us craft undead with certain capabilities that distinguish them from each other or standard ideas.

BODY RESTORATION

First, decide what will heal a body and don't just gloss over this without commenting on it. Is it a potion? A priest? A device? How much healing can be done? If the body is nothing more than ashes because someone burned the body, can the spirit still get the body back? That would be extreme. Less extreme is a body that's been dead a couple days. It arguably takes less power to restore that one.

If the body can only be restored enough to support life but is badly wounded, the spirit will need to address that, and maybe know this in advance and have someone standing by to finish healing it. This would be a standard concern for this particular undead type. Imagine people sighting this undead and realizing that it must be lining up a doctor and how this might affect their decisions to stop it.

What kind of individual would be willing to help our spirit? Family? Someone in it for money? Or being coerced by that spirit? A spirit terrorizing someone into helping carries an interesting side effect—if the undead is brought back to life, it loses its newfound powers (if it had any), and can become vulnerable to the one who has just been terrorized into restoring it. Is the undead character smart enough to foresee such an outcome and take precautions against revenge, keeping leverage that continues into its new life?

BODY POSSESSION

Whether our spirit's own body is available or not, it can try to take someone else's. There are several options to consider here. First, will the new body need to be missing its soul? In this scenario, a smart spirit that is capable of jumping into a body should hover around places where young, healthy people die, like an army in battle. But there's still the problem of inhabiting a body that's now dead, unless this spirit is powerful enough to force locomotion and then get someone to heal it, too. This seems impractical.

Second, if the spirit can take over a body with a soul, what happens to the existing soul? It is ousted or still there but suppressed? The former case causes another spirit to be on the loose. The latter offers an internal struggle; will our spirit be powerful or forceful enough in personality to win or end up the one suppressed but now trapped within someone else? Or can they jump out whenever they want?

IF SUCCESSFUL

An undead who gets itself restored to life faces an interesting prospect. Now what?

If they've got their own body (healed or not), how will people react to this? Will old acquaintances and family have some sense of what's happened? Is this person known to have been dead and then resurrected or is he assumed to have been in an afterlife? The latter suggest a peaceful return and time prior to that. The former suggests sinister, unsettling issues. And what of all their worldly possessions, especially if they've been legally declared dead? Do they have options for restitution? Is our world a place where people return from the dead all the time and have certain rights they can expect? A Bill of Undead Rights is just what the world needs.

If they have a different body, what are they going to do? Embark on a new life as that person or try to reintegrate themselves into their old life as their old self? In the latter case, will anyone believe they're who they say they are? How would people react? Has our undead done anything to prepare for such an issue? Wouldn't it be better if a spirit attempting to do this has made plans for this while still disembodied, and that there's a type of spirit that typically does these things? That makes this less an issue of that character and more a behavior of this undead type.

If they start a new life in the new body, might they run into someone who knew the previous owner of that body? Such a concern could have them moving far away, so have they planned for this? Would our undead be intending to start up a new life and therefore engaging in certain behaviors that are typical of this undead type? Imagine a spirit who can steal gold for their new life, and haunt a place they want to live once they have a body again, driving out the living so no one will take the home until they arrive in their new skin later, buying it with that stolen money. This can be a character, but it can also be a type of undead.

FINDING PEACE

Undead are considered damned to wander for eternity and likely want to be at peace instead. The longer they're undead, the more this could be true, and the more upset they could be. It may not know how to reach this goal. Does our undead seek priests or family members for help? It may not realize the fear it will cause or naively think help will come when an attempt at destroying it might be the result instead, though this could achieve peace of a different sort anyway.

An undead may simply want to be left alone, lying in a grave until compelled to emerge, such as vampires that need to feed. Spirits might want to exist in a perpetual state of denial that they have indeed died, haunting their homes in a dream-like state where the passage of time doesn't register on them, as if they died this morning when decades could've passed. Some might want to simply retrace steps from a happier time and be content with this existence, only to have frightened people interfere with them. Such an undead would be harmless but assumed to be dangerous by those unfamiliar with this type's traits. These are standard ideas.

CAUSING TORMENT

In theory, everyone wants peace, but some enjoy riling up others in life. If they become undead, especially spirits that can appear and disappear at will, tormenting others is easy. This can be innocent fun or an attempt to mentally and emotionally destroy their victim(s). This can be for revenge against just one person or all humanity (or a species).

APPEARANCE

If our undead can only originate in a given way, then they might have a look common to all. We judge and classify by appearance, like it or not. For example, decide that our undead is a skeleton or rotting corpse, not that it's both. The caveat here is that if corporeal undead are created by raising bodies from a cemetery en masse, the result will indeed be a mix of these two, unless a spell or technology used to create them is targeting one type of remains versus another.

Can people tell our undead is undead? With spirits, this is usually obvious, but there are stories of ghosts looking like they're alive. The truth presumably becomes more apparent if contact is made or it does something to give itself away. Or someone gets close enough. If a spirit has the ability to open doors or otherwise interact with the physical world, then it could be virtually impossible to tell what it is. Usually in stories, we want a clue, meaning at least something is a bit off, such as it casting no shadow or being translucent.

For corporeal undead, the presumed answer is that people can immediately tell it's undead. We like the horror a corpse produces, but then vampires are most often shown appearing alive. The degree of decay can be everything down to a skeleton. Many corpses will show evidence of what killed them, including missing limbs or gaping wounds.

A skeleton presumably doesn't carry disease. It wouldn't wield a metal weapon with any skill, for the weapon would slide around in their hand more than a wooden one like a club; this is assuming we care about being realistic. Maybe these undead are really keen on finding gloves to solve such problems and this is an indication of their intelligence and an identifying trait (i.e., a glove-wearing skeleton is type so-and-so); they might also want footwear. Thinking like this is one way to make something more believable.

Skeletons with no clothes imply either being buried

that way or being dead long enough for whatever they were wearing to completely rot or fall away once they rose, so consider having a certain amount of clothing, even armor, on the undead. They can acquire more once moving around, so it makes sense that some of it will have deteriorated (giving a clue what they were buried in) and some will be newer.

TRAITS

The distinction between spirits and corporeal undead notwithstanding, when creating undead, the difference between one and another will largely come down to what they can and cannot do—or even what they tend to be doing regardless of capabilities.

SPEECH AND OTHER SOUNDS

In theory, a corporeal undead would have difficulty talking due to a tongue and more drying out. If a skeleton has nothing to talk with, spirits are even worse off. We may opt to ignore all of this so that they communicate effectively, or give them telepathy. Try to be consistent; if the undead walks funny, it should have trouble speaking clearly. It doesn't make sense for one part of the body to be impaired but another to be unaffected by decay. If we want an undead to speak fluently but have trouble walking, we can fix this by having a leg wound cause the latter.

Completely silent undead or those making tormented attempts at communicating can be more frightening. An undead might be able to say only a few words, and if so, those are probably the ones associated with a goal. This could be the name of their child they want to save (or failed to save), for example. Another option is for it to emit a sound meant to draw others to it or affect them, such as causing a trance-like state in victims. Such a sound would make this undead type identifiable.

TOUCH

Corporeal undead have no trouble touching the world they're still physically a part of, but does their touch corrupt in any way? It can be poisonous, infecting a limb that must be removed. It can just cause unbearable cold that lasts. We can decide it causes the person touched to have visions of what the undead sees, like who its master is, or what it wants, or what horror it faces now. These results and others of our invention can be part of our undead type.

Since disembodied spirits don't inhabit a body, by definition, it's logical that their ability to interact with the physical world is compromised, and yet we've all seen movies where they can move objects or directly touch the living. Sometimes this touch is something they must learn or which takes a toll on them to perform; otherwise it's too easy and they don't have limits on their powers.

Decide how much our spirit can manipulate the physical world, how often, for how long, and to what end. Are they only able to pass through some kinds of objects and not others? Does the material something is made of affect their ability to touch it? Are they only hurt by something like silver? Can they touch people and if so, what affect does that have on the living or the spirit?

The ultimate version of touch is possession of a victim's body. An appealing idea involves the victim gaining the inhabiting spirit's skills—becoming an expert musician or gymnast, for example. A caveat here is that the body won't have the training. The body simply wouldn't be capable of it, but this again depends on how realistic we want to be.

MOVEMENT

The slow-moving undead of yesteryear seemingly paid more attention to realism but has given way to faster-than-humanly-possible corporeal undead. Assuming we want to justify anything, the latter can have either a supernatural, technological, or possibly genetic cause (in the form of mutation). Slow moving ones don't seem frightening anymore unless sheer numbers have blocked escape routes. Today's audiences expect better than victims who just stare in horror until undead surround them.

If we're giving our undead superhuman abilities, a good rationale sells this better. Knowing their origins will help; if a spell designed to grant speed to someone killed them instead, then making them fast in death makes sense. An animated corpse is presumably powered by unholy forces that also allow it to experience little or no fatigue.

Spirits are often shown gliding around or just appearing as if teleporting; the latter suggests knowing they're dead while the former suggests ignorance of this fact. Can spirits pass through objects? If so, this can be because they don't recognize a change has taken place, such as a bookcase being placed in front of a door long after they're dead; doing so might not indicate awareness of their death but being stuck in time, seeing the past instead of the present.

CONSUMPTION

If our corporeal undead needs to consume something to remain animated, is it really dead? Logically the answer would be no, but we accept the idea that vampires need to consume blood, as if a dead body has any ability to process liquids, not to mention oxygen in blood. What else might our undead need to consume? Souls is a good answer, as is energy of some kind. Maybe there's a supernatural substance they need. In SF, this could exist only in space, causing the undead to be a traveler.

If we've invented plants or animals with special properties, perhaps our undead is compelled to feed upon them for some advantage thus gained. Decide if our undead can't survive without it or just gains something else like abilities. Or maybe it uses narcotics to dull the misery it feels. Imagine a drunk undead. Finding that narcotic would give it a goal.

Our undead might be consuming out of habit, as in the case of a primitive, mindless undead. In this case, it may not even be aware that it can't digest food, or that drink just leaks out of its innards. This can give our undead a typical, identifiable appearance—freshly stained with food and drink.

Spiritual undead have no body to consume with, but physical items aren't the only sustenance available. Maybe the spirit wants or needs to feed on emotional turmoil it causes. Or it could drain the life energy from the living. Or devour their soul. It can feed on magic or energy from technology. Are there supernatural phenomenon that attract spirits? Can our species harness those and use them as a lure?

RESIDENCE

Corporeal undead have to be somewhere when not terrorizing people, so decide where it resides. We're looking for a dwelling type more than a specific place, unless we're creating something that's only found in one region of the world. Do they return to a grave or spend time in caves or abandoned ruins? The latter is arguably the most interesting. Undead are sometimes depicted as being only a creature of the night, but they still exist during the day. There's no particular reason they must be in hiding, with one obvious exception—if they're hoping to do bad things without getting caught, fewer people are out at night and they could meet the goal more easily.

Spiritual undead have less need of a residence but are often thought to be tied to a place by sentiment. This is usually a home or the place of a big event, including their death. If they died long ago, other things could've been built there since. In space faring stories, an individual spirit could end up on a ship that takes it away from home but the desire to return home is a character issue, not an undead type.

Aside from the mortal world, is there somewhere they go when not haunting someplace? This is something few creators address. Are they in an afterlife? Do they have any sense of time passing? Are they just dormant like a hibernating bear? While this doesn't need addressing, it could help us imagine something unique.

DEATH

Nothing lasts forever, including undead. Our characters will be highly interested in the question of whether this thing can be eliminated or not, and how to do so, so we'll need an answer.

SPIRITS

The final outcome for a spirit is typically banishment to an afterlife like heaven or hell, unless we have somewhere else to send them, such as a prison for ghosts. That would seem to be a temporary measure, which is fine but suggests unfinished business might come up later. Another option is for a soul to be destroyed, which is very final and not terribly nice. If that spirit was irredeemably evil then this might be fair, but innocent spirits exist.

Achieving the desired outcome is another matter. Does our spirit need to be confronted with a truth to let go of this world? Does it need to be trapped by spells or technology, such as the infamous pentagram drawn on the floor with blood, holy water, or some kind of salt or other material they cannot pass over? Does a priest need to channel the power and word of a god through prayer and blessed objects? None of that is original but if we invent objects required for this, then we turn these into something more unique.

If a spirit has possessed a body and is driven out, decide what happens to the now-vacated victim. Are they insane? Do they return to normal albeit traumatized? Do they have any knowledge of what was going on while they were possessed? Did the spirit communicate with them? Was the spirit able to guard its knowledge and plans from discovery or was the victim privy to knowledge that could be sinister or horrifying? Perhaps the victim knows things they shouldn't. They could now be under the control of the spirit (even though the spirit is gone) via manipulation, threats, or an ongoing compulsion to obey in a Stockholm syndrome sort of way.

CORPOREAL

When destroying corporeal undead, the focus tends to be on the body, with little concern given for what happens to a soul, if one is present. Soul and body are seen as bound so that truly rendering the body unusable is seen as resolving the matter entirely. This needn't be the case, for such a loosed spirit could then become a spiritual undead instead; it may have even started that way before possessing this body.

Entrapping the corporeal undead is theoretically easier, given that there's a body to ensnare and ordinary mortals could do so (or at least think they can). The difficulty may lie in the qualities of the undead we've created: super strength or something so like a wild animal in ferocity or being a disease-carrier. To craft an idea truly our own, we can imbue an ordinary object, such as rope, with a special property that counteracts our undead's unique qualities. Bless it. Irradiate it. Soak it in a chemical or a substance that appears only in space. What danger do these things pose to the living?

Once destroyed, some undead types have a habit of returning to life unless other measures are taken, such as dismemberment, fire, or entombment in a special grave or container. Can ours come back? How can it be stopped for good?

Fire is the stereotypical way to destroy undead, the rationale seeming to be that a dead body is cold and therefore cold doesn't bother the dead. Conversely, heat must. Besides, encasing someone alive in ice will kill them. Doing that to undead will just immobilize them until thawed. Fire will destroy everything but the bones, and if the fire is hot enough, even those can be turned to ash. This is something about the concept of undead that actually makes sense, which can possibly inspire you to invent things that do the same.

WHERE TO START

We should first decide if there's an existing type of undead that we can use or make minor alterations to. If there is, then we likely have some idea what we hope to accomplish. As with monsters, this can involve basic appearance or behavior and imagined scenes of this undead frightening or attacking our characters. Work out these impressions, deciding if this undead has a body or not, and if so, whether there's a soul inside. This will suggest other attributes. Then begin using the template in Appendix 7 to address subjects you haven't considered yet. This can be done in any order, but it's helpful to decide origins before figuring out what it wants, which in turn affects behavior and even abilities. Whether it can be killed, and how, can also greatly affect just how dangerous it really is.

CONCLUSION

I've often joked that I find it hard to believe that God created the world in only six days because it takes me forever. Hopefully this volume will speed you along in your own invention of life. It bears repeating that world building is optional and not everything in this series must be done. Try to avoid feeling overwhelmed. If this happens, take a break. You might be taking everything too seriously. As your world's ultimate god, what you say goes. This includes a decision to skip over the invention of something because you don't need it, don't care, don't have the time, or don't have an idea. This book and the templates should help you flesh out forgotten areas of invention, but it's okay to have blanks in your files where nothing is written about a subject; I have left things this way for over a decade. One day it will occur to you (or not) to write something for that subject, especially when you need it for your project.

Don't let this become a chore. World building is fun.

GOD TEMPLATE

NAME

NICKNAMES/TITLES

Gods usually have one or two titles or nicknames.

OVERVIEW

FAMOUS FOR

Include the god's reputation, that of followers, or both.

DOMAIN

What is the god's chief area of concern (love, war, death)? What other areas help readers or inhabitants understand what this god is like? Are their secondary traits, like a god of love being the god of marriage?

GENERAL DESCRIPTION

In what form does the god appear? Human? Animal? Which gender? Do they have famous objects? Are those feared/coveted by mortals and others?

ALIGNMENT

Is the god good or evil?

SYMBOL

Keep symbols easy to draw, not for your sake, but your characters. Artists can draw more elaborate ones, but your world's residents need something straightforward.

OTHER IDENTIFIERS

Is this a god of an element, season, color, or month?

PERSONALITY

Discuss the god's moods, outlook/vision, friendliness, etc. Mention the god's intelligence, wisdom, and charisma. If it seems appropriate, discuss strength, constitution, agility, dexterity, and morale.

RESIDENCE

Where does the god live? What is it like? Are visitors allowed and under what rules? Who or what else dwells there? Are there guardians? Humanoids? Creatures?

HISTORY AND MYTHS

What has your god done in the past? Created or destroyed lives or items? Fought with other gods? What myths exist about them? Have the humanoid species tried to do things to this god, such as steal a possession, and did they succeed? At what cost?

MYTH 1

Explain your myth or story about this god here and state whether the story is true or not. Is there a moral to the story to instruct the species?

CREATIONS

SPECIES

Which did this god help create? The god's influence on them might be better described in that species' file, but you can say what effect they typically have.

PLACES

Has this god created a place? This could be an island, a forest, building, or sanctuary of some kind.

ITEMS/POSSESSIONS

Has this god created any items for others or themselves? What possessions do they have and what properties (supernatural or otherwise) do they have?

RELATIONSHIPS

FAMILIAL

Are they the parent/child, or sibling of other gods? Do they have half-god offspring? What form do those beings take? A monster? An animal? An intelligent, sentient life? If so, mention them here and use another file to describe those beings in detail.

How old is your god and how does this relate to others (younger, older)?

SPECIES

How do they view and get along with each species?

PATRONAGE

Who does this god support?

CONFLICTS

Has this god participated or abstained from any wars? At what cost, and to whom? How do they typically fight? Can this god be incapacitated or killed? What sort of weapon will do it?

APPENDIX 2

SPECIES TEMPLATE

NAME

NICKNAMES/TITLES

Do they have nicknames?

FAMOUS FOR

Are there attributes that this species is famous for?

GENERAL DESCRIPTION

OVERALL APPEARANCE

Include voice, posture, impression, sleep/eating habits.

THE HEAD

Eyes, brow, ears, chin, jaw, nose, lips, hair styles (and colors), tongue. Heart-shaped, round, square. Bearded?

THE BODY

Discuss height, stocky/thin, details on hands/feet, athleticism, stamina, strength, common ailments. Can include clothing.

SPECIAL

Anything more unique about them, like appendages or supernatural skills.

GODS

Which gods created them, influence them, or are worshiped by them? How does this affect them?

CHARACTERISTICS

INTELLIGENCE

WISDOM

CHARISMA

STRENGTH

CONSTITUTION

AGILITY

DEXTERITY

MORALE

SPECIFIC ACCOMPLISHMENTS

WARS WON AND LOST

INVENTIONS AND DISCOVERIES

WORLD VIEW

CULTURE AND CUSTOMS

Do they work every day? Take lunch naps? Include marriage, death, birth.

SOCIETY

Do they build cities? Scavenge or farm and hunt? Live in tribes?

LANGUAGE

Do they have an oral or written language? Which languages do they typically know?

RELATIONS WITH OTHER SPECIES

HUMANS

SPECIES 1

SPECIES 2

THE SUPERNATURAL

MAGIC

Can they do it? What kind of magic, how powerful can they become? Are they afraid of it?

HABITAT

Where a species lives determines many traits.

TERRAIN

Where do they originate? Land with rolling hills? Mountains? Plains? Forests? The sea? Which is their preference and why? Defense? Food? Overall environment?

CLIMATE

Where are they found? Where are they not found? Are they known for disliking a climate and grumbling about it?

SETTLEMENTS (TOWNS/CITIES)

Creating settlements is discussed in *Creating Places (The Art of World Building, #2)*, but here we can decide overall look, feel, layout, and considerations that distinguish this species' settlements from other species. Decide if they're willing to live in large numbers in joint settlements, abstain altogether, or just have quarters (like the French Quarter in New Orleans) in a joint settlement. Or do they live among everyone?

HOMES

Where are their homes? On land? In trees? Underground? Underwater? How are they laid out and protected? Are homes communal? Are their rooms with special functions, socially or supernatural? Ceremonial? Do they have weapons rooms? Are homes passed down generations? Are any living there?

STYLES & MATERIALS

What are their homes made of? Wood? Brick? Straw?

COMBAT

Do they fight at all or run? How do they fight? With what weapons and armor? Do they use cavalry, dragons? Any typical battle formations?

ECOLOGY

Mating, birth, rearing.

WORLD FIGURE TEMPLATE

———•••———

Use this for heroes, villains, martyrs, and any other famous characters in your world.

NAME

Include proper name and nicknames.

FAMOUS FOR

Summarize in a few sentences what people think of with this person. Details of events and traits are further down. Include legends.

THE FACTS

Are there things believed about him and which are false? Are some things true but doubted? Are some things unknown and would they change anyone's opinion of him?

TRAITS

CHARACTERISTICS

Is this a knight? Star fighter? What profession or trait defines him? What injuries do they bear the scars from?

STATUS

Is he dead (presumed?) or alive? Missing?

POSSESSIONS

Does he have any well-known possessions like a magic sword, dragon, well-known horse or ship? Why and what?

FAMILY

Are his parents around? Any children? Does he know he has children? What are their relationships like? A hero might have earned enemies that go after family. A villain might have killed theirs or been disavowed by them. Are parents or children old enough to interfere with his plans or life?

RELATIONS WITH SPECIES

How does he get along with each of the species? More importantly, is he viewed differently by each species, or famous for different things?

HISTORY

ORIGINS, DEMISE, AND IN BETWEEN

Where is he from? What formative events made him who he is? Where did he live? Is he there now? If he's dead, where are the remains and his possessions? Is the grave protected? Dangerous?

TRAINING AND SKILLS

How did he get his skills? Innate? Training? Life experience? What are the rumored and real sources of personality traits or skills that led him to become famous?

CREATING LIFE

THE DEEDS

Tell us what this character did or achieved and how. Why did he become famous? Was there a reason no one else could do it or was this just the first one to do it.

Monster Template

---•••---

MONSTER NAME

The monster might have a name it thinks of itself as, and another that others call it.

NICKNAMES/TITLES

Do they have nicknames?

FAMOUS FOR

If the monster is known to exist, is it famous? This suggests it's hard to kill because quite a few people probably would've tried, and failed, by now.

DESCRIPTION

What does it physically look like? Does anyone ever get a good look at it? Are stories about it exaggerated? How does it feel about its appearance and how people react to it? What sorts of stories do people tell about it?

MOTIVES

What does your monster want? To be left alone? Hoard treasure? Food? Security? Revenge, and for what?

ORIGINS

Did someone create this monster on purpose or by accident, or is it a product of nature?

GODS

Does the monster recognize or worship any gods? Or work with them? Receive aid in return for something?

CHARACTERISTICS

INTELLIGENCE

How smart is it? Is its intelligence limited to things like hunting, and is that just instinct more than thought? Some monsters aren't much smarter than animals, but monsters who were once human, for example, can be very smart.

WISDOM

Monsters aren't known for wisdom, but is it wise enough not to step into obvious traps? Does it know better than to go into town and kill people because a bunch of people will come to kill it as a result?

CHARISMA

Monsters are usually called that for being hideous, but not always. Some are beautiful or have the ability to convince people they are with hallucinations or illusion.

STRENGTH

Monsters are often depicted as stronger than most other beings, so just how strong is this one?

Constitution

Does the monster have an unusual ability to withstand pain? Can it travel farther and faster than its pursuers without exhaustion so that tracking it is hard? Does it withstand wounds in combat, or heal faster?

Agility

How mobile is it? Fast or slow? Does its body hinder movement or help it? Can it chase down prey or flee those chasing it? Is it faster than a horse?

Dexterity

How much control does it have with weapons or tools?

Morale

Monsters are usually the ones scaring everyone else, but is there anything the monster is afraid of? Does it flee from battles when too many are against it or is it fearless?

WORLD VIEW

What is the monster's viewpoint about itself, others, and its place in the world?

Society

Monsters are generally isolated and have no society of their own, but what about the monster's impact on a nearby society? How is it thought of? Does it impact life there, such as people not traveling in its direction (or taking special precautions)?

LANGUAGE

Does the monster speak any known languages or is it reduced to grunts like an animal? Is it easy or impossible to understand? Can it read and write? If so, someone had to teach it, so who did that? That individual has befriended the monster and likely protects it, but possibly doesn't want that known.

CUSTOMS

Is there anything that the monster does that could be considered a custom or habit, such as stacking the bones of victims? Or displaying them? Does it attack at a certain time of the month, year, or decade?

RELATIONS WITH SPECIES

If the monster has a unique relationship with a given species, list it here. Also, how do the different species view the monster? Do some want it left alone while others want it killed? Captured? Enslaved?

HUMANS

ELVES

DWARVES

DRAGONS

OGRES

SKILLS

What can your monster do that is unusual? What is normal for a creature with its limbs and their physical features to do but this monster *cannot* do?

THE SUPERNATURAL

Is the monster supernatural in any way? Can it perform magic? Is it afraid of magic? Does it have a supernatural place nearby? Does it utilize it or avoid?

FOOD

What does the monster eat? How often? Are species on the menu? Why does it eat them (just for food or to induce horror)? Does it lure food to it or hunt it?

HABITAT

Does the monster have a lair? What is it like? Are there bones lying around—or even arranged neatly like trophies? Does the monster stay in its lair most of the time? Is it mobile within the lair? How far from its lair does it travel? Does it have more than one? Is it a wandering monster with no home? Is it looking for one now? Does it prefer a particular type of place (cave, abandoned city)? Is the monster nocturnal?

COMBAT

How does the monster fight (which body parts are used—arms, legs, tail, teeth)? Does it use brute force? Cunning? Stealth (stalking prey)? Does it lure victims into a trap? Does it have any special attacks or tricks it can use?

ECOLOGY

Is the monster capable of reproduction? How often? How many offspring are produced at once? Are they born in an egg? Are they like sharks and immediately dangerous? How does it reproduce? Sex? By itself? Can it mate with species or animals and if so, is the result the same kind of monster or a hybrid? Has it ever reproduced? Is this monster the offspring of something?

Plant Template

———•••———

PLANT NAME

Description

What is its climate, season, appearance, texture, toxicity, smell, feel, and taste? When is it planted, grown and harvested?

Uses

How is this plant used? What products are made with it?

Reputation

Are there any stories about it, whether harvesting difficulties or famous/infamous uses?

Analogues

What Earth equivalents exist? This isn't something to tell your audience but helps you easily remember what you were thinking.

ANIMAL TEMPLATE

———•••———

Use this for mammals, birds, fish, amphibians, and reptiles.

ANIMAL NAME

What does it look like and how does it behave? How is it used?

TYPE

Mammal, bird, etc.

MATING/BIRTH

Do they lay eggs or have live birth? What's the litter size? How long does it take? Do the mothers raise the young and for how long?

LIFESPAN

HABITAT

Does it prefer mountains, forests, deserts?

CLIMATES

PLACES FOUND

What are some specific places it's found, such as a kingdom or forest?

Solitary or Pack?

Prey

Herbivore, carnivore, or omnivore? If the latter two, does it eat animals or also species?

Predators

Do species prey on this animal? For trophies, furs, teeth, poisonous spines? To capture and breed them? Do your species eat it?

Analogues

What Earth animals is this similar to? This is something for your private notes more than to tell an audience, as you can't compare your world's animals (or anything else) to Earth unless the characters have been here.

Undead Template

------ •••• ------

UNDEAD NAME

DESCRIPTION

What does it look like? Does it appear alive or obviously dead? If a spirit, does it retain a self-image of itself as healthy and alive as if its unaware of its death, or does it's self-image reveal it knows (such as a gaping wound)?

TYPE

Animal, plant, humanoid; spiritual or corporeal (with or without a soul?).

LIFE CYCLE

ORIGINS

What caused this type of undead to exist? An accident? If so, when did it happen, why, and who caused it? If someone invented the undead on purpose, why and how did they do so?

REPLICATION

How many of them are there? Can it make more of itself? How long until someone/something else becomes one once exposed to the triggering incident? How long does something have to be dead before becoming this?

DEATH

Can this undead be destroyed for good? How? What happens to it? If not, what happens when attacked with enough force to seemingly kill it or render it immobile? Does it recover, and if so, after how long?

HABITAT

Does it prefer graveyards, the wilderness, or abandoned homes or those lived in?

PLACES FOUND

What are some specific places it's found, such as a kingdom, city, or forest?

SOLITARY OR PACK?

Is it found in groups, alone, or both? If a pack, can the pack communicate and move as if they're of a shared mind?

BEHAVIOR

CHARACTERISTICS AND SKILLS

What can it do and not do? What hurts it? How strong, fast, smart, and agile is it? Can it speak, read, write, and understand the living or dead? Can it perform magic? Do biological scanners and other devices work on it? Can it use them (like a fingerprint scanner)? Spirits can move through objects or touch them. Undead can withstand some forces or not.

MOTIVES

What does it want? If it gets this, does it stop?

PREY

Does it have anyone in particular it preys upon? The innocent? Those of a certain religion or with none? What does it do to victims? Turn them into one, use them like a parasite would (such as feeding on them but leaving them alive), or just kill them?

COMBAT

How does it fight? With weapons held in the hand, its body, or thrown objects? What hurts it? What cannot hurt it? Does it gain power from certain kinds of attacks, as if feeding off them?

BIBLIOGRAPHY

AAPA (1996). "AAPA statement on biological aspects of race" (PDF). *Am J Phys Anthropol*: 569–570

Apse, Will, "Types of Plants (With Pictures)," *Owlcation*. Owlcation.com, 8 JUN 2016, Retrieved 10 SEP 2016.

Arnold, Nicholas; Ovenden, Denys (2002). *Reptiles and Amphibians of Britain and Europe*. Harper Collins Publishers. pp. 13–18.

Beneski, John T. Jr. (1989). "Adaptive significance of tail autotomy in the Salamander, Ensatina". *Journal of Herpetology*. 23 (3): 322–324.

Biodiversity Institute of Ontario; Hebert, Paul D. N. (October 12, 2008). "Amphibian morphology and reproduction." *Encyclopedia of Earth*. Retrieved August 15, 2012.

Broome, Tom, "Introduction to Cycads," *Iris Online*. IrisOnline.com, Retrieved 28 DEC 2016.

Cartmill, M. (1985). "Climbing". In Hildebrand, M.; Bramble, D. M.; Liem, K. F.; Wake, D. B. *Functional Vertebrate Morphology*. Cambridge: Belknap Press. pp. 73–88.

Davis, Mark; Everson, Michael; Freytag, Asmus; Jenkins, John H. "Unicode Standard Annex #27: Unicode 3.1," Unicode.Org, 16 MAY 2001, Retrieved 15 APR 2016.

Dorit, R. L.; Walker, W. F.; Barnes, R. D. (1991). *Zoology*. Saunders College Publishing.

"Dwarfism," *WebMD.com*, WebMD, LLC, Retrieved 1 MAR 2016.

King, Gillian (1996). *Reptiles and Herbivory* (1 ed.). London: Chapman & Hall.

Garnett, S. T. (2009). "Metabolism and survival of fasting Estuarine crocodiles". *Journal of Zoology*: 493–502

Gill, Frank (1995). *Ornithology* (2nd ed.). New York: W.H. Freeman.

Hey, J., "The mind of the species problem." *Trends in Ecology and Evolution*: 326–329. 1 JUL 2001, Retrieved 12 JUN 2016.

Hildebran, M. & Goslow, G. (2001): *Analysis of Vertebrate Structure*. 5th edition. John Wiley & Sons Inc., New York.

Huey, R.B. (1982): "Temperature, physiology, and the ecology of reptiles." In Gans, C. & Pough, F.H. (red), *Biology of the Reptili* No. 12, Physiology (C). Academic Press, London.

"Long-distance Godwit sets new record". BirdLife International. 4 May 2007. Retrieved 13 December 2007.

"Introduction to Marine Mammals" and "Taxonomy," *MarineMammalCenter.org*, Marine Mammal Center, Retrieved 27 DEC 2016.

Leonard, Scott A; McClure, Michael (2004). *Myth and Knowing* (illustrated ed.). McGraw-Hill.

Mishra, S.R. (2005). *Plant Reproduction*. Discovery Publishing House.

Nelson, Joseph S. (2006). *Fishes of the World* (PDF) (4th ed.). John Wiley & Sons. Retrieved 30 APR 2013.

O'Grady, Stephen E., "Basic Farriery for the Performance Horse," *Veterinary Clinics of North America: Equine Practice*, Volume 24, Issue 1, Pages 203-218

"Plantigrade," *Wikipedia*, Wikipedia Foundation, Inc., Retrieved 8 JUL 2016.

Pitcher TJ and Parish JK (1993), "Functions of shoaling behavior in teleosts," *Behavior of teleost fishes.* Chapman and Hall, New York, pp 363–440.

"Reptile and Amphibian Defense Systems". Teachervision.fen.com. Retrieved March 16, 2010

Robert, Michel; McNeil, Raymond; Leduc, Alain (January 1989). "Conditions and significance of night feeding in shorebirds and other water birds in a tropical lagoon" (PDF).

"Sentience," *Merriam-Webster.com*, Merriam-Webster, Retrieved 23 DEC 2016.

Stebbins, Robert C.; Cohen, Nathan W. (1995). *A Natural History of Amphibians.* Princeton University Press.

Speaksman, J. R. (1996). "Energetics and the evolution of body size in small terrestrial mammals" (PDF). *Symposia of the Zoological Society of London*: 69–81.

Spearman, R. I. C. (1973). *The Integument: A Textbook of Skin Biology.* Cambridge University Press. p. 81.

Sullivan, Brian K. (1992). "Sexual selection and calling behavior in the American toad (*Bufo americanus*)". Copeia.

"The Difference Between Annual Plants and Perennial Plants in the Garden," *The Garden Helper*, Retrieved 22 JUN 2008.

Thompson, Helen. "What's the Difference Between Poisonous and Venomous Animals?" *The Smithsonian Mag*, Smithsonian.com, Retrieved 24 JAN 2017.

Toft, Catherine A. (1981). "Feeding ecology of Panamanian litter anurans: patterns in diet and foraging mode". *Journal of Herpetology.* 15 (2): 139–144.

Toledo, L. F.; Haddad, C. F. B. (2007). "Capitulo 4". *When frogs scream! A review of anuran defensive vocalizations* (PDF) (Thesis). Instituto de Biociências, São Paulo.

"Warm and Cold-Blooded," *CoolCosmos.ipac.caltech.edu*, CalTech, Retrieved 28 DEC 2016.

Willmer, P., Stone, G. & Johnston, I.A. (2000): "Environmental physiology of animals." *Blackwell Science Ltd*, London.

Womack, Mari (2005). *Symbols and Meaning: A Concise Introduction*. AltaMira Press.

"Why are most Semitic languages written from right to left, while European languages are written left to right?," *Quora*. Quora, Retrieved 12 JUN. 2016.

About the Author

Randy Ellefson has written fantasy fiction since his teens and is an avid world builder, having spent three decades creating Llurien, which has its own website. He has a Bachelor's of Music in classical guitar but has always been more of a rocker, having released several albums and earned endorsements from music companies. He's a professional software developer and runs a consulting firm in the Washington D.C. suburbs. He loves spending time with his son and daughter when not writing, making music, or playing golf.

Connect with me online

http://www.RandyEllefson.com
http://twitter.com/RandyEllefson
http://facebook.com/RandyEllefsonAuthor

If you liked this book, please help others enjoy it.

Lend it. Please share this book with others.
Recommend it. Please recommend it to friends, family, reader groups, and discussion boards
Review it. Please review the book at Goodreads and the vendor where you bought it.

JOIN THE RANDY ELLEFSON NEWSLETTER!

Subscribers receive discounts, exclusive bonus scenes, and the latest promotions and updates! A FREE eBook of *The Ever Fiend (Talon Stormbringer)* is immediately sent to new subscribers!
http://www.ficiton.randyellefson.com/newsletter

OTHER RANDY ELLEFSON BOOKS

TALON STORMBRINGER
Talon is a sword-wielding adventurer who has been a thief, pirate, knight, king, and more in his far-ranging life.

The Ever Fiend
The Screaming Moragul

There will be many more of Talon's stories, which can be read in any order. To see a suggested reading order, which updates each time new stories are released, please visit www.fiction.randyellefson.com/talonstormbringer

THE ART OF WORLD BUILDING
This is a three volume guide for authors, screenwriters, gamers, and hobbyists to build more immersive, believable worlds fans will love.

Volume 1: *Creating Life*
Volume 2: *Creating Places*
Volume 3: *Cultures and Beyond*

To learn more, please visit www.artofworldbuilding.com

RANDY ELLEFSON MUSIC

INSTRUMENTAL GUITAR
Randy has released three albums of hard rock/metal instrumentals, one classical guitar album, and an all-acoustic album. For more information, streaming media, videos, and free mp3s, please visit http://www.music.randyellefson.com

2004: *The Firebard*
2007: *Some Things Are Better Left Unsaid*
2010: *Serenade of Strings*
2010: *The Lost Art*
2013: *Now Weaponized!*
2014: *The Firebard* (re-release)